UNLOCKING
WORLDS

UNLOCKING WORLDS

A Reading Companion for Book Lovers

SALLY ALLEN

Griffins Wharf Productions
Westport, Connecticut

Griffins Wharf Productions
Westport, Connecticut

First published by Griffins Wharf Productions, 2015.

www.griffinswharfproductions.com

www.sallyallenbooks.com

ISBN-13 9780983644613

ISBN-10 0983644616

For Henry,
with whom I've shared many magical reading adventures

"the great advantage of being a literary woman was that you could go everywhere and do everything."
– Henry James, *The Portrait of a Lady*

TABLE OF CONTENTS

INTRODUCTION

Readers, Readers Everywhere

*"Ah, how good it is to be among
people who are reading."*

– Rainer Maria Rilke

It was on a crisp, late winter morning that I found myself pausing in the driver's seat, keys in hand. I was meeting a friend for coffee, and my current read, Donna Tartt's *The Goldfinch*, was sitting on the passenger seat looking, with its worn and torn dust jacket, like a sad little puppy that doesn't want to be left behind during a shopping excursion. To bring or not to bring? I'm not above reading at inappropriate moments, but really.

Of course I brought it with me. When deep into a great book, a need possesses me to carry it with me wherever I go, never to let it stray too far from my thoughts or person. Also, I was at a particularly compelling point in the narrative. What if the line was long or my friend was late? What if an asteroid hit the parking lot just exactly where I had parked my car? It's best not to take any chances.

Later, with *The Goldfinch* tucked in my purse and parked on the seat next to me, I was explaining to my friend my strong conviction that books and reading can be galvanizing forces for community and connection. This point is beautifully illustrated on page four hundred sixty-three in *The Goldfinch* (hardcover edition): *"[S]he had only to mention a recently read novel for me to grab it up hungrily, to be inside her thoughts, a sort of telepathy."*

At this moment in the story, Theo, the narrator, is referring to the woman he is in love with, but his idea could apply more broadly, to family and lovers and friends and complete strangers, including those we'll never meet. The shared experience of a book is the shared experience of a world. When we hold it in our hands, we hold at least one commonality, a magnetic pull that prevents us from floating out and away and alone into the ether, a gravitational force rooting us to solid ground.

Not a minute later, a complete stranger who was approaching the café's coffee line exclaimed with delight at *The Goldfinch's* spine peeking out of my purse. Then she looked at me with a smile best described as radiant. A brief but enthusiastic exchange about the book's merits ensued, with another person on line chiming in—*How far along are you? It just gets better and better! I never wanted it to end!* The Goldfinch!

"See what I mean?" I said to my friend.

Despite the illusion that reading is solitary, we readers are always in conversation—with books, of course, but also with other readers and critics, especially now. When I was growing up and becoming a reader, reading recommendations and conversations about books revolved around librarians, teachers, friends, and my parents or siblings. In other words, people who knew me reasonably well. Besides trusted recommendations, I chose books based on whether I liked how they looked and read them before knowing anything about them beyond the publisher's description printed on the back cover. While the characters, places, and experiences that books connected me to stretched far beyond the boundaries of my real life, the readers to whom books connected me were part of my world in a very immediate sense.

Now, before ever laying eyes on a book (never mind cracking it open), I can go online and find hundreds, even thousands, of faceless, disembodied readers—about whom I know virtually nothing and who know nothing about me—critiquing and otherwise commenting on it. Besides volume, variety is also at my fingertips. The dialogue around books is nothing if not diverse in subject matter and approach: top five, seven, or ten lists, snarky jibes or encomia, serious long-form criticism or quick capsule reviews, quizzes to determine which literary character or book I am, and everything in between. And authors are part of the conversation too, not only through the traditional routes of author talks and readings but through social media, allowing me to connect and even converse with them from anywhere in the world. It can feel overwhelming, but it's also exhilarating. So much time, thought, and creative energy, and it's driven, at least in part, by passion for books and reading.

This passion is what I wanted to tap into by studying literature at the university level. I spent the summer before college fretting about what I would study, and what I would do with my life. For ideas, I turned to books (of course), notably the cheerily titled *Careers for Bookworms & Other Literary Types*. My brother seemed to think my way forward was clear. "You like to read," he said. "Why don't you major in English?"

I *did* like to read, though this strikes me as a kindly understatement. Actually, I hoovered books and would read anywhere, anytime, including, memorably, during my best friend's eighth birthday party. I like to blame my reading obsession on my parents, not because both are prolific readers (though they are) but mostly because they did not allow me to watch television. Evenings would not find us gathered in front of the screen as a family, debating what to watch, which is understandable when one considers that my mother referred to TV as "the devil."

We did own one for the utilitarian purpose of watching the nightly news and for my father, a devout New York Giants fan, to follow his favorite team's exploits. But if my mother caught my siblings and me (transgression was best practiced in group form) watching television, she would holler, "Turn off the devil!" Except it sounded more like, "TURN OFF THE DEVIL!" Also, she said it in Greek. As hilarious as it was to provoke this outburst for its pure absurdity (can you imagine if it were actually possible to "turn off" the devil, just shut that sucker down with the flick of a switch?), the television was best left alone. This left me with unclaimed hours to fill. Theoretically, I could have occupied myself with any number of activities: sports (but I don't like to sweat), piano (but my mother insisted I practice half an hour everyday, greatly reducing its appeal), drawing. Actually, I rather enjoyed drawing, but not as much as getting lost in books.

Right around first grade, I experienced a moment of existential crisis. I was standing outside my parents's home listening to the kids who lived across the street playing in their front yard. There were seven of them, one boy, who was the oldest, and six girls. Though I adored my siblings, we were not close enough in age to be playmates, and as the youngest, I often felt like a bit of a hanger-on. Plus everyone was always *shushing* me. As I gazed up at the house where I lived, listening to the neighbors, thinking how fun it would be to have an in-house playmate (or six), it occurred to me: *I am the only me there is. I can never know what it's like to see what someone else sees or live anyone else's life or think anyone else's thoughts. Just mine. All I can ever be is me.* This realization was a depressing blow, unanticipated cloud cover intruding on what had been a limitless blue horizon.

As fate would have it, I had recently discovered that the lines and squiggles sweeping across the pages of my schoolbooks were symbols for words that coalesced and bloomed, powered by my imagination, into characters, scenes, ideas, worlds. Books became my portal to new points of view, new places, new friends, new experiences. Though they were virtual, and thus not as ideal as, say, trading bodies with one of the kids across the street for a day (as Annabel and her mother trade bodies in Mary Rodgers's *Freaky Friday*), books were my next best option. And I threw myself into reading, gobbling up books as if my life depended on it. And maybe in a sense it did. My favorite characters were friends and confidants who inspired, advised, and consoled me. With books, I was rarely lonely and never bored. When I could get away with it, I would read under the covers with a flashlight long past my bedtime. As a backup option, I created my own audiobooks by recording myself reading my favorite books so I could listen to them on my headphones. I even sketched pencil drawings of my favorite characters and wrote lost chapters featuring me as the plucky friend. So yes, you could say I liked reading.

Armed with my brother's suggestion and my trusty copy of *Careers for Bookworms* (now in its fourth edition), I earned a M.A. in English Literature and a Ph.D. in English Education, with an emphasis in writing and went on to teach writing, literature, and communication. By the time I graduated and was well into my teaching career, I discovered another outlet for sharing my passion for building community through reading and books: book blogs. Blogging about books introduced me to a new world of book lovers and connected me with passionate readers across the globe. Closer to home, that experience segued into writing about books and authors for a local news website, and eventually, I founded Books, Ink at HamletHub, a website devoted to sharing local happenings for book lovers in Connecticut.

What You Will Find in This Book

"What is literature?" The professor who would eventually become my dissertation advisor posed this question in one of my early doctoral seminars, a course on theories of reading. We graduate students were seated in chairs forming a cozy little circle, perched at the edges of our seats, eager to share our clever, insightful responses.

> *The characters seem like real people.*
> *The reader misses them after the book is over.*
> *The narrative is complex.*
> *The story stays with you.*
> *The language is beautiful.*
> And so on and so on.

"But who gets to decide whether a book possesses these qualities?" our professor further inquired. His question was followed by a lengthy pause, throat clearing, general fidgeting, and possibly a tumbleweed or three. We had, it seemed, been led down a garden path to ruin. He answered his own question then: "If a reader has these experiences with a book, then that book is literature for him or her."

Given my populist sensibilities, I liked his answer very much. At the same time, I understand why it makes some people uncomfortable: It suggests that standards and categories don't matter. But I don't believe this was my professor's point. I believe he was getting at something more difficult and more humane: Standards matter, but people matter more. Many or most of us would probably acknowledge that books exist along a continuum of bad to great. It's just that absolute literary value isn't always relevant to a reader, unless that reader happens to be creating educational curricula or sitting on a prize committee panel.

For readers—and here, I'm referring to those of us who choose to spend time with books for pleasure and/or enrichment—what matters is the experience of a book, whether that book blossoms in our imaginations, whether we connect with the characters, whether the events in the story resonate, inspiring us to think and feel. Making such an experience possible requires considerable effort and skill on the parts of *both* author and reader. But here's a shocker: We will never, ever (unto eternity) all agree on which books best succeed at making these experiences possible, no matter how discerning the reader or brilliant the text.

When I set out to write about the books I have read and valued, I wanted to capture both the enjoyment and enrichment that attend reading books of all kinds and for various reasons. These happen when we take the time to listen to what a book has to tell us—whether it's a quick read, a compelling classic, or a big book that challenges our modern-day limited attention spans but promises richness and a depth of experience. I wanted to acknowledge the personal nature of book preferences and to write about books in a way that seeks to enlarge and enrich rather than merely assess. I also wanted to present the books spoiler free (with one notable exception, about which you will be duly warned).

I've organized the eighteen chapters as follows: Chapter One lays out my beliefs and values about reading, the ones that shape my book preferences and assessments. Chapters Two through Sixteen are organized around themes and subjects that I find myself returning to again and again. Each chapter begins with my reflections (as a reader and human) on the significance of its theme and/or subject and includes my discussion of ten related reads. The books I discuss aren't meant to represent a definitive list of What To Read. They're books I've read in recent years and valued, books that resonated and stayed with me, and books that reward generous readers. In these reflections and discussions, I hope readers will discover new books or shared experiences of familiar ones and inspiration for reflecting on the preoccupations that shape and have been shaped by their favorite reads. In Chapters Seventeen and Eighteen, I explore the joys of living a bookish life, even when we're not actually reading a book.

CHAPTER 1

Let Reading Change You

*"There is creative reading as
well as creative writing."*

– Ralph Waldo Emerson

I don't read for the same reason each time I pick up a book. At any given time, I may read for any one or combination of the following:

To understand the past
To understand my own time
To understand myself
To understand others
To get lost
To be challenged
To relax

What I'm reading for and why influence how I assess a book's merits, and the same book can be more and less relevant at different stages in my life. Just because a book is deemed "good" or even "great" does not mean that I will be in the frame of mind to receive it. So many great books exist and continue to be written that it seems an ill use of emotional energy to feel badly about the ones I don't personally connect with or like, as long as I understand that whether I like a book has little, if any, relevance to its literary merit.

Similarly, it's possible for me to enjoy or find value in a book but still recognize it as something other than a great literary work. While reading a book that seemed unremarkable, I've stumbled on an emotional truth that, for completely personal reasons, gave me a way to make peace with a difficult experience, and this has salvaged the book for me. For this reason, the writing about books I find most helpful to read and that I prefer to write revolve around the potential meaning I can take from a reading experience.

It's important to me to be transparent about the qualities I ascribe to "good" and "great" books. And all of the reads that I take the time to discuss in this book are those that have been, to some extent, satisfying, enjoyable, and/or enriching and that feature, to varying degrees, the following five qualities.

Compelling Narrative voice. A compelling narrator pulls me into the characters's experiences, no matter how foreign they are from my own, and inspires me to feel empathy. Whether the voice is playful, melancholy, angry, humorous, etc., if I can connect to the characters's experiences, I can submit to the story. This doesn't mean the narrator must be trustworthy. Take Sophie Kinsella's *Shopaholic* as a light-hearted example. It's clear that the narrator cannot be trusted because we, the readers, are given evidence that contradicts what she says about herself and her experience. A large part of the book's humor is grounded in that disconnect between what the narrator believes about herself and what we know about her based on other evidence presented to us. The success of that humor lies in the reader "getting" that she is an untrustworthy narrator, and part of what inspires empathy for her is recognizing her struggle to face her own flaws. However, when I am meant to trust the narrator and don't, because my interpretation of events is at odds with the book's as a whole, I tend to feel unsatisfied and frustrated.

Purposeful Shaping of Language. An author's use of language is the medium through which readers access and identify with characters's experiences. In *Infinite Jest*, for example, David Foster Wallace uses sentence fragments, excess verbiage, and narrative disconnect to unsettle and confuse the reader, which brilliantly echoes, at the sentence level, the protagonist's experience in the moment. It may be frustrating to read, but it's intended to be so because the frustration we experience enables us to identify with the protagonist's experience. For me to call a book "good" or "great," this purposeful shaping of language to some degree is a "must have." Sometimes this means language that creates the illusion of seamless beauty, and sometimes, as in Foster Wallace's case, it means language that challenges us. One of my preoccupations is improving my ability to communicate, and to do so requires understanding language's infinite potential. I appreciate authors who show me that potential.

On the other hand, a book overpopulated by cliché expressions and/or generalizations tends to bore or frustrate me because I don't feel that I'm learning anything new about either language or the experiences being described and explored. When authors find new ways to express universal experiences, my understanding of those experiences deepens. Here is one of my favorite examples, from Vladimir Nabokov's *Pnin*: *"His life was a constant war with insensate objects that fell apart, or attacked him, or refused to function, or viciously got themselves lost as soon as they entered his sphere of existence."* Now imagine if he had just referred to Pnin as "clumsy" and "absent-minded." These adjectives capture the gist of Pnin's experience in the physical world but without painting the tragicomic portrait of him as a hapless victim of objects conspiring against him. Not quite the same effect, eh?

Purposeful Ambiguity. When a novel is open-ended or a character's decisions can be both justified and criticized, I call this purposeful ambiguity, meaning it mirrors a reality of life: It generally refuses to be as tidy and clear-cut as we may wish it were. In Sophocles's tragedy *Antigone*, for example, Antigone cannot deny her brother a proper burial, and Creon cannot allow her to bury him. Competing roles and responsibilities compel each to act in ways that are irreconcilable with the other. In this extreme example, it is also tragic. I do not believe a book has to be tragic to be good, but a good book, for me, acknowledges life's gray areas, its moral, emotional, and spiritual struggles. Good books raise important, often difficult, questions and invite us to think through them. When *ambiguity* devolves into *confusion*, with storylines disappearing halfway or three-quarters through, never to be mentioned again, or being resolved too simplistically or in contradiction to the reality established in the book's world, I am left feeling unsatisfied and frustrated.

For some readers, any type of hopeful or positive ending, the type typical of romantic comedies for example, is rejected as being "unrealistic," "implausible," and/or "simplistic." I am not one of those readers. The work of living is, to me, the work

SALLY ALLEN

of choosing to find meaning, purpose, and hope. I appreciate authors who understand that we are always making choices and who show me what it looks like to choose meaning, purpose, and hope even, and especially, when it is most difficult. For examples of books that do this in a satisfying way, I recommend J. K. Rowling's Harry Potter series and *All the Light We Cannot See* by Anthony Doerr.

Emotional truth. It's a delicious paradox that good books express universal human experiences by sinking deeply into individual characters's inner lives. The deeper they go, the more likely they are to reach the core of what it means to be human. This is why we can read literature written from a different time and place—Charles Dickens or Petrarchan sonnets or ancient plays—and shiver with recognition. This is how books help us understand experiences we have not had and people we have not been, thus enlarging our capacities for empathy. Even when the packaging may be unfamiliar (i.e. Dickens's Pip in *Great Expectations*: An orphaned blacksmith's apprentice in Victorian England receives an anonymous inheritance) the underlying emotional experiences are familiar (i.e. the thrill of reinvention erases old loyalties, or we don't know how to value what we have until it's lost).

Books I'm likely to call "good" or "great" feature characters whose inner lives not only resonate—regardless of whether those characters and I have anything in common other than that we are both human beings—but also reveal the emotional truths that cause or alleviate suffering. "Bad" books, not so much.

Wholeness. In a good book, everything serves a purpose, and the end of the book seems self-evident, even if we didn't predict it or we wished the character's story ended differently. Consider the first *Harry Potter* novel.

Spoiler Alert: I'm about to discuss the ending of *Harry Potter and the Sorcerer's Stone* novel. If you have not read the book and do not want it to be spoiled, skip to the next paragraph.

The narrative led us to suspect that Snape was trying to kill Harry, but at the end, when it is revealed that it was actually Voldemort acting through Quirrell trying to kill Harry, we look back at all the clues we relied on and realize our sources were flawed. We read the clues from Harry, Ron, and Hermione's points of view, and we got the facts wrong because they did. When the truth is revealed, it is connected to previous evidence that we (and they) misread.

A book can lead me along a false trail, but if the ending doesn't come together in a way that is plausible and evidenced, if the events and their resolution seem random and disconnected, I feel dissatisfied and frustrated. These feelings of dissatisfaction and frustration may lead me to not like a book.

But I might also not like a book that I recognize is beautifully written and/or thought provoking and/or skillfully executed. And sometimes, because I enjoyed spending time with them and was glad to have read them when they were over,

I love books that probably will not end up in The Canon of Great Literature. In short, deciding whether a book is good or bad is not the same as deciding whether I liked it.

As a teacher of writing, literature, and communication, I have come to believe that understanding ourselves and others and learning how to express ourselves productively to each other can alleviate a great deal of human suffering. Consequently, whether I like a book is not as important to me as whether it teaches me to be a more empathetic human being.

Before I leave you to it, I want to share a work that has profoundly influenced how I aspire to read (and live): a breathtakingly beautiful essay called "Criticism" by Matthew Goulish, author of *39 Microlectures: In Proximity of Performance* and co-founder of Goat Island (1987) and Every house has a door (2008). "Criticism" explores the function of criticism and its effects on the critic, and I have found its ideas broadly applicable to teaching, writing about books, and living.

Goulish writes, *"Whatever we fix our attention on seems to multiply before our eyes. If we look for problems, we will find them everywhere. Out of concern for ourselves and our psychic well-being, let us look instead for the aspects of wonder."* I want to slow down and linger here for a moment: *"If we look for problems, we will find them everywhere."* Have you ever found this to be true? I certainly have. We live in an imperfect world, so of course we can't avoid finding problems. They really *are* everywhere. I would say it then logically follows that problems will be fairly easy to spot, and so it's not terribly intellectually taxing to build a practice around the act of rooting them out.

In the years since I first read Goulish's essay, the phrase *"aspects of wonder"* has stuck with me like peanut butter to the roof of my mouth. I have found it a sane and humane way to enter an artistic (or other) experience and also more nourishing. But it's more challenging as well, all the more so because we're often taught to assess a student, a text, a relationship, a life in negative terms, meaning in terms of what is absent rather than of what is present. I've begun to wonder if perhaps we're taught to find problems because they're easier to locate and talk about than *"aspects of wonder."* The latter evokes an earnestness that's often frowned upon in a cynical culture where "appreciating" is suspiciously close to "liking," which is often viewed as a lack of judgment or critical acumen. But as I've said above, appreciating and liking are not synonymous experiences. And liking, or loving, or enjoying doesn't necessarily point to an inability or lack; it takes a keen mind and an open heart to recognize and value beauty.

Goulish also points out that criticism rarely changes the art it critiques. In the case of books, if I write a bad review detailing everything wrong with a book, does this change the book itself? Is the author going to revise it based on my criticism and then re-release it? Well, no, obviously. So then who or what is actually changed by my criticism? According to Goulish, it's me, the critic, who is primarily changed by my engagement with a book: *"Criticism only consistently changes the critic,"* he writes, *"whether further narrowing the views of the art policeman, or incrementally expanding the horizons of the open-minded thinker."* This means each of us has the power to let ourselves grow from a book (or artwork), but we need to understand that the decision—and responsibility—is ours.

I can't leave Goulish behind without mentioning this salient observation of his that expresses one of my core values: *"[E]ach work of art is at least in part perfect, while each critic is at least in part imperfect."* This is one of my favorite things to remember—as a reader and as a human being. We are all flawed, yet we can create beauty. And this reminds me that the kind of reader we are connects to the kind of person we are in the world. We bring to books expectations, desires, judgments, and personal stories that shape our reading; recognizing this allows us to take responsibility for ourselves, rather than holding someone else responsible for our good or bad time. Reading to understand an author's project, regardless of whether we like that project or not, allows us to practice reaching beyond what we know to discover other ways of looking at the world. And reading for *"aspects of wonder,"* rather than rooting out flaws for the sake of it, allows us to become co-creators of beauty and meaning.

In saying this, I don't mean to suggest that flaws are non-existent or that every book can be satisfying, if only we could see its potential. But if we aggressively seek out imperfections with a single-minded intensity, we risk closing ourselves off from what a book has to tell us. I want to encourage readers to embrace, as they read, this basic challenge of living: To find, amidst the wreckage of the human condition, moments of beauty, connection, and hope.

CHAPTER 2

Beloved Vintage and Classic Children's Books

"No book is really worth reading at the age of ten which is not equally – and often far more – worth reading at the age of fifty and beyond.

– C. S. Lewis

I forget the names of streets, people, books I meant to read. I lose my keys, my mobile, and my shoes on the regular. The name of my first grade teacher, the year we went to the Grand Canyon, the countries my pen pals came from, the address of my elementary school—all have slipped through the gaps of my imperfect memory. And yet, I can recall the names of my favorite childhood books and their protagonists as if I read them yesterday. Perhaps because I was young and impressionable, or perhaps because I read my favorite books again and again, I often remember the made-up stories and people I read about as a child better than I do the events of my real life.

Returning to these childhood worlds as adults can remind us of the lessons we learned and parts of ourselves we may have long forgotten. The following ten books inspired me, as a child, to stretch beyond the limits of my world and the people within it. They inspired me to turn to books again and again and still. And they speak to the power of a good story not only to resonate over the years, no matter who or what we become, but also to continue inspiring us.

A Bear Called Paddington by Michael Bond

Bond's *A Bear Called Paddington* follows the misadventures of a bear from Peru who is discovered wandering through the London Paddington train station. He is found by the Browns (parents Henry and Mary and their children Jonathan and

Judy), who recognize that an impressionable bear needs looking after. They take him in and name him for the station where they found him. In each episodic chapter, Paddington sets out to do a kind turn, with unintended consequences. My affection for this well-meaning but bumbling bear and the family that loves him contributed to my growing up to become a bit of an anglophile. I suspect it's also why, in college, I was determined to spend my junior year in London. Imagine my delight when my assigned housing landed me walking distance from London Paddington! You can try anyway, but chances are, you will underestimate it. Technically, Queensway was the closest station to my flat. But I'd often go the extra distance just to walk in the footsteps of one of my favorite protagonists.

As a little girl, I felt a deep kinship with Paddington, though he was a bear from Peru who lived in London and I was a human girl who lived in New York City. Paddington always tried so hard to do the right thing and yet always seemed to make such a mess. This was how I often felt, and still do, about the difficulty of realizing our best intentions. I say "our" because is this not true of humanity in general? Paddington's struggles are universal, I daresay.

Bond's stories bloomed from a moment of sympathetic identification. While shopping on Christmas Eve in 1956, he saw a small toy bear left alone on a shelf and, feeling sorry for it, bought it as a present for his wife. He named it Paddington for the station they lived near at the time and began writing stories about the bear for fun. Ten days later, he had written a whole book's worth. Bond's compassion for a lonely little stuffed animal resonates in the empathetic stories he spun, which often involve Paddington having to seek forgiveness. And they rather inspire *me*, even today, to strive for compassion, empathy, and forgiveness.

A Little Princess by Frances Hodgson Burnett

While Paddington inspired me to feel compassion, *A Little Princess* showed me how to put it into practice. The novel tells the story of young Sara Crewe, who is brought to London by her widowed father, a British soldier serving in India, so she can attend a boarding school for girls. Sara was a character with whom I felt the strongest affinity from the earliest pages. Like me, she loved her father, books, and her special doll, who Sara liked to imagine could animate and live a full and interesting life when separated from her (I couldn't believe my secret fantasy was right there on the page!).

But these similarities are trifling compared with what Sara's adventures and actions helped me understand: Qualities I might have thought of as flaws—a strong will, a hot temper, pride, a highly articulated sense of justice—are transformed into potential strengths (with the possible exception of the hot temper). Sara is treated like a princess at the boarding school, given the best of everything, and aspires to behave like a princess too, in the best ways possible. She befriends the girls others overlook or mock, treats everyone graciously and politely regardless of their class or their treatment of her, and comforts the neglected. She loves reading, spinning elaborate stories, and underdogs.

The true test of Sara's character is not revealed until after a dramatic change of fortune. Her father dies, suddenly and pennilessly, having lost all his money in a risky diamond mine venture. Sara is moved from her suite of rooms to a garret, fed as little as possible, and put to work running errands and teaching the younger children. Like the scullery maid, Becky, Sara becomes the person others abuse to relieve their own frustrations. In these moments, Sara showed me that being strong-willed could also mean having the will to survive hardship. Sara's story does not end there, but I will let you discover that part for yourself.

Rereading *A Little Princess* as an adult, I noticed troubling details that escaped me as a child, primarily involving imperialism, assumptions about class, and the implications of that diamond mine venture. But I can never forget how meeting Sara taught me about agency, self-control, and care for others in a way I had not been able to articulate before sharing her journey. Her story expressed core values I have tried to live up to ever since: What matters most is what we do with what we have, and our character is revealed not through abstractions and words or by what qualities others ascribe to us, but through our own actions and choices.

All-of-a-Kind Family by Sydney Taylor

All-of-a-Kind Family was the first in a series of autobiographical novels Taylor penned about the adventures of five sisters growing up in Manhattan (and later the Bronx) at the turn of the twentieth century. Ella, Henrietta (Henny), Sarah, Charlotte, and Gertrude (Gertie) were named for Taylor's real-life sisters, with middle daughter Sarah bearing Taylor's birth name (she apparently changed it in high school).

I loved all the books in the series, but the one I spent the most time with as a child was the first, which features twelve vignettes, each a chapter, that build to reveal a mystery. Along the way, we meet Miss Allen, the librarian at the girls's local branch of the New York Public Library, who teaches Sarah that taking responsibility for her lost library book will require personal sacrifice but also enable her to continue enjoying what she and her sisters love: reading. We visit Papa's junk shop, populated by colorful characters and revealing unexpected treasures. We discover that, sometimes, a scavenger hunt can transform an unpleasant task into a game. We learn how Jewish and American holidays were celebrated a hundred years ago, including Purim, Sukkot (spelled "Succos" in the novel), Passover, and the Fourth of July. We visit Coney Island and the market and celebrate a new arrival. And we work out that, sometimes, you have a bad day, but it passes, partly through the support of those who love you and partly because you decide it's time to let go.

Though the ending reveals the answer to a question running through the individual stories, contemporary readers expecting to be propelled through a nail-biting plot will not find it here. Those who appreciate character and setting, who revel in vibrant details that craft a finely wrought portrait, and who possess a curiosity about the past will find this book a treasure. Rereading it recently, I fell in love with it all over again. Our world has changed dramatically and rapidly over the last hundred years, but the values Taylor illustrates—personal responsibility, the interdependence of the individual and society, and the privileging of people over things in the pursuit of happiness—hopefully will never pass away.

From the Mixed-Up Files of Mrs. Basil E. Fankweiler by E. L. Konigsburg

As a kid, I read and reread Konigsburg's *From the Mixed-Up Files of Mrs. Basil E. Frankweiler* until the covers were tattered. It tells the story of twelve-year-old Claudia Kincaid who runs away from home with her nine-year-old brother Jamie and his well-fed piggy bank. The two decamp from their hometown of Greenwich, Connecticut to the Metropolitan Museum of Art in New York, where they sleep in the museum's fancy bedrooms, bathe in the fountain, and raise funds by collecting coins from said fountain (which, sadly for those wishing to retrace Claudia and Jamie's steps, no longer exists). They also discover a mystery and go to great lengths to solve it.

It's one of the first books I remember loving so much that I wanted to live in it, and many of my recreational hours were devoted to writing the book's "lost chapters" in which Claudia and Jamie are joined on their adventures by a spunky friend (i.e. me). Claudia's journey taught me lessons specific to childhood, notably that growing up is scary. But the book also holds in its pages timeless lessons for any age: We don't have to be stuck where we are but can choose to see possibilities, to create the world we want to inhabit. Finding one's place in the world involves a constant negotiation between the needs of the self and the needs of the community. And while sacrifices will be required, it's okay to want something of one's own to cherish.

Starring Sally J. Freedman as Herself by Judy Blume

Blume's books have ushered more than one generation of children into adolescence and adulthood. My favorite growing up was *Starring Sally J. Freedman as Herself,* set in 1947. Blume, who was seven years old when World War II ended, refers to it as her most autobiographical novel. It does indeed star the eponymous Sally J. Freedman. The book covers ten-year-old Sally's memorable winter in Miami Beach, where she has moved with her mother, grandmother, and brother, Douglas, to help speed up his recovery from nephritis. The children's father visits from their full-time home in New Jersey when possible.

Sally was a kindred spirit in whom I could find refuge. I identified with her spirit of curiosity, her sometimes too vivid imagination, and her superstitiousness. The novel isn't particularly plot-driven. It's more a study of a young girl growing up and into herself, which was comforting for me as a child. Rereading it as an adult, I noticed references and implications that I had missed, as if they were built-in to entice adults to revisit the novel or to entertain them while reading along with their kids.

Like in *From the Mixed-Up Files*, I rather wanted to live in the novel and experience what it was like to use inkwells and write letters and ride trains on long journeys. I'm sure the book sparked my interest in historical fiction (and, to some extent, time travel … and also trains), and I know it inspired my fascination with (and romanticizing of) the 1940s. The still functional vintage 1940s radio I keep on my nightstand and wake up to every day is the visual evidence of this fascination, along with my preoccupation with World War II novels.

Little Women by Louisa May Alcott

Alcott's now-iconic novel features my favorite literary mama, Mrs. March. The mother of Meg, Jo, Amy, and Beth is raising her four daughters alone while her husband serves as a chaplain in the Union army during the Civil War. She devotes her time to charitable causes, takes food off her own spare table to feed others with greater needs, and provides firm but gentle counsel to her girls. The only potential downside to Marmee (as she is affectionately known to her daughters) as a role model is that she sets the bar so darn high!

But I often take heart from remembering that Marmee's good sense comes from self-reflection and correction, revealed after Jo, furious with Amy for burning Jo's only copy of her book, nearly lets Amy drown. As Jo tearfully confesses her fear that her temper will lead to devastating consequences if she doesn't learn to control it, Marmee reveals her own life-long struggle to manage her quick temper. This self-disclosure is an inspiring reminder that we can strive to do our best, even when it's most difficult and even though we won't be perfect.

Though the book is what I would fondly call wholesome, it's not free of mistake making, temptation, and pain. The girls's passage into adulthood involves, in large part, learning to master their personal limitations—impatience, materialism, vanity— and realizing their best selves as often as possible. In this sense, the book brims with timeless wisdom and inspiration. Though the chapters build on each other, they are largely episodic, the better for dipping into and out of as needed.

Mary Poppins by P. L. Travers

Mary Poppins was the first in Travers's series about an English nanny with magical powers. In the popular imagination, fresh-faced Julie Andrews, she of the dulcet tones, lives on as Mary Poppins. But the novel's version of the mythical nanny is much more fearsome, more mercurial, and considerably more vain. She is prone to sniffing contemptuously, giving in to fits of bad temper, and lingering in shop windows to admire her reflection. Yet Mary Poppins is widely revered, which may be one reason her ego is out of control. And not only by her young charges, Jane and Michael, who tiptoe around her moods, always hoping to cajole her into another adventure. Her beau of sorts, Bert (memorably portrayed by Dick Van Dyke in the film), her Uncle Albert, the animals in the zoo, the birds in the sky, and even the wind itself fawn over Mary Poppins.

As I child, I was enchanted by the magical adventures. Like the children in the book, I was puzzled about the identity of this mysterious figure, while also being simultaneously frightened of and fascinated by her. I did so wish to possess the ability to step into a beautiful chalk drawing, as Mary Poppins does on an outing with Bert, or to have tea while bobbing gently near the ceiling, or to speak the same language as animals, or to glue stars onto the night sky. The story's whimsy enchanted me (and still does), but one thing I missed as a child was the book's humor. I laughed out loud rereading it, especially at the absurdity of Mary Poppins's narcissistic self-obsession.

So many of the novels I loved growing up featured children I identified with, values that resonated, and adventures

I might have liked to enjoy personally. I didn't particularly relate deeply with any of the characters in *Mary Poppins*, and it wasn't a novel that, as the saying goes, taught me how to live. But by golly, it was a grand adventure!

Charlotte's Web by E. B. White

White's beloved classic shows young, old, and every age in between how to live in a world that is both beautiful and harsh. The book's first line — *"Where's papa going with that ax?"* — is grounded in the latter. Eight-year-old Fern asks the question of her mother as they prepare their breakfast table (note the smell of bacon wafting through the room). When Fern learns the ax is to slaughter a little pig, the runt of his litter, she rushes out to save him, and she succeeds. Her father gives Fern the pig, which she names Wilbur, to raise until he is big and healthy enough to move to her uncle's farm down the road ... where he will eventually be slaughtered. But at the farm, Wilbur is befriended by Charlotte, a clever spider who is ruthless with her prey but devoted to her new best friend. And she hatches a plan to save Wilbur's life for the second time. To succeed with her plan, Charlotte must use her cunning and enlist the help of other animals who live on the farm, including Templeton, a rat who can only be prevailed upon to help through appeals to his self-interest.

What drew me into the story as a child were the strong interspecies friendships, the charm of talking animals, the excitement of the fair where Wilbur is entered in a competition. It's only now, rereading it as an adult, that I see how elegantly it instructs us—about the importance of recognizing both limitations and strengths of self and other when forming alliances, the need to work both with those we value as friends and those of whom we are wary, and the power of both community and personal responsibility when facing life's harsh realities.

The Little Prince by Antoine De Saint-Exupéry

I have always known my parents to be explorers, and from a very young age, I traveled with my family at least twice a year, during winter holidays and over the summer, in the States and in Europe. Along the way, I developed a love of the journey itself—from deciding what to pack, to hanging out at the train station or airport (especially the airport!), to the time spent on planes and trains themselves. This was a large part of what drew me to Saint-Exupéry's melancholy story as a child: The Little Prince journeys to different planets, and what he encounters along the way nurtures personal growth and learning.

A pilot has crash-landed in the Sahara desert. As he is working on his plane, he meets a fellow explorer, the Little Prince, a small boy from a tiny planet far away. The Little Prince left his home, and the fussy rose he tended on it, in search of something more, something different, something *grand*. He searches, traveling from one planet to another, finally landing on Earth, where he shares his story with the pilot (who in turn shares it with us).

Without spoiling it for those who have not yet read it, the book explores a simple truth that is all too easy to overlook, that value lies not in a thing itself but in our relationship to it. Which is to say, as the Little Prince learns, *"Anything essential is invisible to the eyes."*

Time at the Top by Edward Ormondroyd

My first encounter with time travel literature was when I read Ormondroyd's *Time at the Top* as a kid, a slim volume that packed quite a wallop for me. It was most certainly the first book that made me fall in love with the idea of time travel and with nostalgia as a state of being.

The novel opens on a mysterious note, with police, and an author named Edward Ormondroyd, investigating the disappearance of young Susan Shaw. It all seems terribly sinister, but it's not so much. Susan has traveled back to 1881, courtesy of her apartment building's elevator and a stranger's enigmatic gift of thanks. In the past, Susan finds adventure and friendship, and possibly even family, if only she can convince her father to travel back with her.

The novel does not feature the familiar risks of time travel in that Susan doesn't meet her ancestors or endanger her future self. For her, returning to the past represents a return to a simpler, more romantic time, which accurately captures how we tend to think of the past even now.

CHAPTER 3

Novels That Play with Time and Space

"A great book should leave you with many experiences, and slightly exhausted at the end. You live several lives while reading."

– William Styron

Where books like *All-of-a-Kind Family* and *A Little Princess* awakened in me a curiosity about the past, Ormondroyd's *Time at the Top* made me wish I too could find a magical portal through time and space. When I look back at my past from the present moment, it presents as a braid of interlocking events, each experience, even those I didn't particularly enjoy living through, leading me inextricably to where and who I am now. Because I am reasonably happy with both, it's hard to have regrets, but it can still be tempting to imagine, *What if this one thing never happened? Then where would I be?* We can never know whether pulling out just one narrow thread would cause the whole of our lives to collapse or transform into a more perfect form. This is also true of history: Who can say for certain whether eradicating one wrong-headed decision, policy, or person would solve problems or simply create different problems? Still, the notion that perhaps life and the world could be changed for the better makes time travel a compelling concept; it expresses a faith in the possibility of human progress, as opposed to stasis or regress.

Since I have yet to discover a time machine of my own, I am drawn to novels that play with time, like a bee to honey or a moth to flame, depending on whether one wishes to see the impulse as sweet or destructive. Both sweetness and destructiveness play into the following ten novels in which authors riff on our notions of time in a number of ways. Maybe the hook is that a character relives the same day or series of days over and over until some cosmic wrong or imbalance is corrected.

Maybe a character travels out of his or her time, disrupting the space/time continuum, putting him- or herself in danger of never existing. Whatever the conceit, traveling behind or ahead of the present moment can prompt reflection on what it might mean to live to the fullest in the right now. If you can suspend your disbelief in the mutability of time, these ten novels will offer the opportunity to re-see the present moment in profound and surprising ways.

Before I Fall by Lauren Oliver

This young adult novel begins on a very dark note: Seventeen-year-old Samantha, a lieutenant in a mean girl clique, dies in a drunk driving accident after a night of partying. After her world goes dark, she wakes up to discover she is starting the same day all over again, with the second version ending very much like the first. The time loop continues for seven days until she comes to understand and fulfill the purpose of her repeated returns. In the process, she uncovers secrets that explain (but do not excuse) why her friends are who and what they are.

The action builds to a conclusion that is perhaps unexpected but that also promises hope for redemption, though not in the way that we might wish for in a perfect world. But of course, the world is devastatingly imperfect, and so we are obliged to find what hope and redemption we can, though it leaves us heartbroken. A provocative book for teen readers, it's also just an all-around compelling read.

The First Fifteen Lives of Harry August by Claire North

What if you could do not just a single day, as Samantha does in *Before I Fall*, but your whole life over again and again, and again, ad infinitum? This is the premise behind *The First Fifteen Lives of Harry August*, written under the pseudonym of Claire North (who, because we can't leave well enough alone, has been revealed to be British author Catherine Webb).

Harry is an ouroboron, meaning "cyclical": He is essentially immortal but trapped within roughly the same stretch of years. Born in England in 1919, he lives about seventy-five to eighty-five years and always dies of the same disease, no matter what adjustments he makes to his standard of living. When he dies, he returns to the beginning of his life, regaining consciousness of his memories around the age of four years old.

Searching for answers to explain his condition, Harry discovers the Cronus Club, a group of fellow ouroborons who pledge not to change the course of large-scale events and instead focus on protecting each other and facilitating each member's multiple returns. The book provides thought-provoking portraits of how Harry and others handle their particular brand of immortality. In this sense, *Harry August* is a philosophical novel. But then Harry meets Vincent, an ouroboron who rejects the Cronus Club's pledge to remain on the edges, and who wants Harry to join him in challenging the self-imposed limits of power, knowledge, and control. As Harry wrestles with Vincent, the lure of absolute knowledge, and the impending end of the world, the novel morphs into a page turning thriller with a science fiction bent.

As already noted, time-bending fiction requires a hearty willingness to suspend disbelief. If you're the type of reader who scours a text for leaps or gaps in logic, you might notice a few of them here. I would hazard to say they're inevitable given the paradoxes the conceit invites. All this aside, the novel is an ambitious, expansive, and inventive twist on time loop narratives.

Life After Life by Kate Atkinso

The title refers to the many lives of Ursula Todd, who we meet at her birth in 1910, which she experiences over and over again, with different outcomes. Like Harry in *The First Fifteen Lives of Harry August*, Ursula lives in a time loop, though her awareness of this reality emerges across lifetimes rather than over a few years within a single life. We follow Ursula on her repeated life journeys, including her brush with influenza, married life (and not), and World War II experiences. Her intuitive knowledge about what to do (and not do) builds with each go-round and allows her to make small shifts that lead to global life changes. This raises fascinating questions about the implications of our decisions and actions and makes *Life After Life* a novel I couldn't stop thinking about for a long time after I finished it.

Though the content is heavy, Atkinson is exceptionally witty in a stiff-upper-lip British way, and her characterizations are deep and intricate, making it easy and enjoyable to get lost in her descriptions. Bookish types may especially appreciate how Ursula frequently quotes literature during seminal moments. This quoting echoes the novel's theme of recurrence: Literature often gives voice to our universal human experiences, a language for understanding and creating meaning of those experiences. In this way, *Life After Life* reminds us that we are not the first and will not be the last to feel what we feel.

Kindred by Octavia Butler

Butler was a renowned science fiction writer, winner of Hugo and Nebula awards, and the first science fiction writer to receive a MacArthur Fellowship. She described *Kindred* as a *"grim fantasy"* because she did not use science to explain how protagonist Dana, a descendent of slaves and slave owners, travels back in time from 1976 Los Angeles to 1820s Maryland.

The novel begins with Dana waking up in a hospital after her arm has been amputated. The injury was sustained, we learn, during her most recent return from the past, in which she found herself on the banks of a river, where a little boy, Rufus, was drowning. After pulling him from the water, she was confronted by his enraged father, who aims his rifle at her. In that moment of intense fear, Dana returned to her present.

This first trip initiates a cycle. Rufus, Dana's great-great grandfather and the son of a plantation owner, calls her back to the past each time his life is in danger. She saves him many times over knowing that if he does not live to have a relationship with her great-great grandmother Alice, Dana will not be born. As her trips extend for greater and greater lengths of time and put her in increasing danger as a black woman in the antebellum South, the compromises she must make to survive compel us to ask: How does one preserve a sense of personal agency, autonomy, and dignity within a system that denies it?

The lyrical restraint of Butler's prose wields a hypnotic power in this devastating read that explores the paradox of coming to terms with an irreconcilable past.

1Q84 by Haruki Murakami

Murakami's haunting novel, about a parallel world as opposed to a future or past one, begins in 1984, with Aomame, a personal trainer with a unique and sinister talent, stepping out of a taxi stuck on a jammed expressway. She emerges, like a modern-day Japanese Alice in Wonderland, into a world whose incongruities gradually reveal a cavernous fissure between the world she inhabits—which she dubs 1Q84, the 'Q' representing the question of where she is—and the one she left behind. We then meet Tengo, a math teacher who, like Aomame, is nearing thirty, experienced isolation and loneliness as a child, and gets sucked into a subversive scheme that threatens to undo the carefully regimented world he constructed for himself. Their stories are told in alternating chapters that grow increasingly suspenseful as the reader works to piece together how they are connected. Like Aomame trying to make sense of the incongruities in her new world, we become detectives of a sort, sifting through lush details in order to determine which might be clues to the bigger picture.

As with Murakami's other novels, longing and sadness permeate the world he has crafted. But his descriptions of emotional truths are so devastatingly on target that it's almost impossible to feel alone reading his novel. How can we feel alone and isolated when the author is describing those precise emotional experiences as though reading our minds? Even though the tension became almost excruciating, I found myself slowing down as I got closer and closer to the end, not wanting my time in the world of 1Q84 to end.

Landline by Rainbow Rowell

Rowell writes lovely, heartening novels for both teens and adults. *Landline*, which falls in the latter category, follows the time-travel(ish) awakening of Georgie McCool, a Los

Angeles-based comedy television writer. Georgie plans to head to her husband Neal's Nebraska hometown for the holidays with their two daughters. But a week before their trip, she receives the opportunity of a lifetime: her own show. The catch? She and her writing partner must produce four scripts in ten days.

Stay-at-home dad Neal, once a comic illustrator/writer and aspiring oceanographer, refuses to cancel the trip and leaves with their girls. Brooding and anxious that Neal's departure may not be temporary, Georgie retreats to her mother's house. There, she discovers an old rotary telephone that connects her to Neal ... in 1998, the year the couple wrestled with whether to continue their relationship or part ways for good. As modern-day Georgie revisits old battlegrounds with 1998 Neal, she is reminded of the compromises both have made, forcing her to reckon with their choices and to question the 1998 breakup-that-wasn't.

Rowell has a uniquely tender narrative voice, one lacking sharp edges and dark alleys. Yet with all its compassion and gentle humor, *Landline* asks difficult questions and resists easy resolutions: If given an opportunity, what would we change about the past, if anything? And if we change one thing, how does that affect all the other parts? The novel is about reckoning with the choices you've made, the life you've created, the need for risk, and the impossibility of perfection.

Here I Go Again by Jen Lancaster

Lancaster's books—fiction and memoir—tend to be conversational, silly (in a good way), amusing, and upbeat. What I most love about her memoirs is how charmingly self-deprecating she is. She can poke fun at herself, though it's clear she has a strong sense of self. These qualities carry over entertainingly into her fictional protagonists.

At thirty-eight, Lissy Ryder has hit a low point. The queen bee of her high school is facing her twenty-year reunion having lost her job, her home, and her husband and unable to understand why. At the reunion, she encounters a girl she once bullied, who grants her an opportunity to return to the past to right her wrongs. The novel takes a few unexpected and thought-provoking turns, and in one of the more imaginative scenes, shows how it's possible to wake up in 1991 instead of 2011 and not realize it right away. Also, the pitch perfect ending made me laugh out loud.

The Map of Time by Felix J. Palma

Nothing is quite as it seems in this three-part novel that defies our expectations and keeps us constantly on our toes. Intricately plotted and expansive, reading this novel is like entering an enormous maze. You might think you've arrived at the center only to realize you've gone down another dead end. Time to double back again. Another angle from which to view events lies in wait, another perspective to be discovered, another possible set of outcomes.

Set in late nineteenth century London, the book introduces us to a cast of characters who appear and reappear when we least expect them, including H. G. Wells. His *The Time Machine* functioned as a kind of cautionary tale about the consequences of putting too much faith in science. The fictionalized Wells is the centripetal force around which *The Map of Time*'s plot spins.

This is the kind of book that makes you realize that everything is connected, if only by the thinnest of threads. And beneath the vast web of interconnected characters and stories lie crucial questions: What happens when we believe that time travel is possible? If we could travel through time, would we be able to solve problems, right the wrongs of the past, our own and history's? Where is hope to be found? Is it in science or in our own imaginations? If time is not a straight line that moves in only one direction but instead is a mutable, nonlinear boundary, what becomes of individual will?

The Future of Us by Jay Asher and Carolyn Mackler

Two teens get a peek at their future in this young adult novel. The story begins in 1996 with high school junior Josh taking a brand-new AOL CD across the street to Emma. The two were best friends until he misinterpreted her feelings and tried to kiss her, and nothing has been the same between them since. Meanwhile, when Emma puts in the CD, she discovers a website called Facebook, where she can read snippets of her future self's life. And she doesn't like what she finds. Josh is also on Facebook in the future, and he thinks he likes where he ends up. But as the two begin to alter their presents in anticipation of their futures, they're forced to rethink their choices and confront their nascent selves.

I loved the idea of this novel, especially as it's targeted to Millennials whose lives are increasingly mediated through technology. My favorite moment in the book is on page thirty-two (paperback edition), when Josh and Emma are reading status updates: *"'Why would anyone say this stuff about themselves on the Internet? It's crazy!'" 'Exactly,' I say. 'I'm going to be mentally ill in fifteen years, and that's why my husband doesn't want to be around me.'"* But if we are being honest, couldn't we all do with a reminder to drag our eyes away from our screens and engage with the big, messy, three-dimensional world?

The Impossible Lives of Greta Wells by Sean Andrew Greer

With emotional acuity and delicately crafted prose, Greer explores the pressures that different realities, expectations, and political climates bring to bear on the individual. The novel opens in 1985, where thirty-two year-old Greta Wells loses her twin brother, Felix, and descends into a debilitating depression.

Her relationship with Nathan, her love of ten years, breaks up. Her brother's lover, Alan, is also dying. Her greatest source of solace is her Aunt Ruth, who lives in the apartment below hers in Greenwich Village.

The eponymous "impossible lives" are three time periods through which Greta cycles—1985, 1918, and 1942. Her time travel—which is not only to the past but to alternate realities—is spurred by the electroconvulsive (in 1985) and electroshock (in 1918 and 1942) therapy her therapist recommends to ease her depression. In each time period/alternate reality, she is the same person, living in the same apartment, and part of the same family. But she, Felix, Alan, and Nathan face discrete challenges that invite us to ponder the extent to which we are shaped by our age and the extent to which we can shape the world into our ideal image of it. For Greta—as for us—the trick is in identifying what she can control and grabbing it fearlessly, without looking back.

CHAPTER 4

Travelers's Tales

"You forget everything. The hours slip by. You travel in your chair through centuries you seem to see before you."

– Gustav Flaubert

S ome of my earliest memories are of traveling from New York to Athens, Greece. These memories come to me in images, snatched from the precipice of my unconscious. I remember waking up after an uncomfortable night folded into my airplane seat, disoriented and mildly nauseous and looking out the window at the city below. Unlike the gleaming silver skyscrapers of my native New York, Athens unfurled in low, uniform buildings, tightly packed and spread across hills and mountains. At the airport, I remember food carts that offered "toast," which was not, as it was at home, toasted bread but toasted bread with cheese, and possibly ham. Small bags of potato chips clipped to the cart advertised flavors I'd never imagined—hot dog, paprika, feta. Outside, assaulted by the acrid smell of exhaust and choking smog so thick it was almost visible, I felt the vastness of the unknown world and the smallness of me within it. It was not so much frightening as it was thrilling. So many mysteries to uncover and explore! This was my first realization of the way fine details that make up everyday life—the landscape, scents, food—eventually melt into background material, barely worthy of notice. But when traveling beyond everyday boundaries, even the familiar becomes new (hot-dog-flavored potato chips!).

This prompting of awareness to the everyday is the promise of travel: to shelve our expectations and reckon with what we take for granted. Along with the things around us, we may then also experience ourselves as new, discovering unrealized potential, renewed enthusiasm, untold strength. Such is the case with the travelers in these ten stories, whether their journeys are literal or figurative. And they might just inspire you to embark on your own journey of discovery, whether by foot, plane, train, or through the pages of a book.

The Unlikely Pilgrimage of Harold Fry
by Rachel Joyce

One of my calming pre-flight rituals is to buy a book in the airport bookstore. When I chose *The Unlikely Pilgrimage of Harold Fry*, it was because it seemed symmetrical to read about a man embarking on a journey when I was also about to embark on a journey. Recently retired Harold Fry lives a staid, predictable life in an English village with his wife Maureen until the morning he receives a letter from Queenie Hennessy, a woman he'd worked with many years before. Queenie has written, she tells him, to say goodbye. She is in hospice care on the other side of England, dying of cancer. Harold pens a brief note to her, but when he walks up the road to drop it in the post box, he finds it too inadequate a gesture and decides to walk a little longer and think a little harder. From one post box to the next he goes until, after stopping at a gas station for refreshments, a conversation with the station attendant inspires Harold to walk across England to go to Queenie's side. *"Wait for me,"* he writes on the outside of the note he originally penned, before finally dropping it into a post box.

The book follows his progress and the insights he gains about himself and about life during his journey in this poignant, heartfelt, and beautiful meditation on who we become and how to recover a sense of faith and possibility.

American Gods by Neil Gaiman

American Gods won the Hugo Award for Best Science Fiction/ Fantasy, the Bram Stoker Award for Best Horror Novel, the Locus Award for Best Fantasy Novel, and the Nebula Award for Best Novel. Since horror, fantasy, and science fiction are pretty much the last genres I'm likely to gravitate to, I figured I should read *American Gods*. Like ruts of all kinds, I try to avoid reading ruts, when I can.

Newly released from jail, Shadow believes he is on his way home to his wife and a job with a friend when he meets Mr. Wednesday. An improbable series of circumstances arise that result in Shadow taking a job with Wednesday and traveling America on a mysterious mission. Mystical happenings, macabre humor, and ancient legends, vendettas, and beings collide as the novel snakes its way towards a potentially grim conclusion.

It's a novel that's hard to pin down and that requires submitting to the experience to appreciate, which I did. Once I gave in to the story's flow, I was drawn in and glad I had pushed myself out of my genre comfort zone. If you don't mind not knowing what's going on *at all times*, the rhythmic prose will carry you along to the end, where the novel's internal logic reveals itself. As a bonus, the Tenth Anniversary Edition features material that was not included in the original.

Americanah by Chimamanda Ngozi Adichie

You know those books that absorb you into their worlds from the very first page? This was one of those books for me. The story is told from the points of view of Ifemelu and Obinze, who meet and fall in love as teenagers in Nigeria but travel down very different paths on the way to adulthood. Ifemelu leaves Nigeria to attend college in the U.S. while Obinze stays behind, eventually spending three ill-fated years in England before returning home.

The story begins fifteen years after Ifemelu first arrived in the U.S. as she travels from Princeton, where she has a fellowship, to Trenton to have her hair braided at an African salon. During her trip, we learn that Ifemelu has achieved success as a blogger about race. Her anonymous blog is called, *"Raceteenth or Various Observations About American Blacks (Those Formerly Known as Negroes) by a Non-American Black."* It chronicles her experiences and observations from the point of view of an immigrant—she does not disclose, in the blog, where she is from—who never defined herself in terms of race until she moved to the U.S. When we meet her, Ifemelu has decided to shut down her blog and return home. As she sits in the Trenton salon, her early life and years in the U.S. unfold in flashbacks. Obinze's experiences on the other side of the world unfold parallel to Ifemelu's.

We follow their first meeting and the decisions that separated them, both physically and emotionally. We follow the friendships that sustain and challenge them in Nigeria and abroad. We follow important moments in their lives as each moves forward, including Ifemelu's early struggles in the U.S., her two significant relationships with American men, her success as a blogger and speaker, Obinze's troubled years in England, and his difficult return and eventual personal and career successes. And we follow Ifemelu after she returns to Nigeria and begins her new life there.

Though there is suspense regarding if and how Ifemelu and Obinze will cross paths again, this is not a plot-driven novel. It renders deeply felt characters living complicated lives, wrestling with difficult questions, struggling to do the right thing and to figure out what the right thing is. At turns funny, philosophical, heartbreaking, and intellectual, it is a meditation on first love, on race and class in the U.S. and U.K., on living in a Third World country, on immigration, and on finding home.

Le Freak: An Upside Down Story of Family, Disco, and Destiny by **Nile Rodgers**

Forget whatever assumptions you may have about music industry memoirs and the glorifying of hedonism. This is a book about the art of making music, from developing an idea to executing it and all the steps in between. It's also about Rodgers's journey and how his passion for music has saved him many times over. *Le Freak* tackles his experiences chronologically, beginning with his turbulent childhood and moving through his career milestones. Besides his own band, Chic, he has produced some of the biggest names in the music industry, including Diana Ross, Duran Duran, David Bowie, and Madonna.

The book is beautifully crafted. Rodgers has a great instinct for when to delve into the sensory, providing metaphors that kept me engaged and able to identify with the emotional truths of his experience, which are, as in any successful memoir, both specific and generalizable. Once he gets into the music industry part, it was almost like reading a mystery; I was propelled through the plot, anxiously waiting to see what happens next. Rodgers clearly loves what he does, does it well, and knows how to talk about it so that a lay audience can relate.

I loved his generous, uplifting spirit and his ability to find meaning in even the most painful parts of his journey. If you like to feel good and read smart, well-written memoirs, read this book.

Paris to the Moon by Adam Gopnik

This memoir is like the clown car of memoirs, except instead of clowns stuffed into a car, it's rich, fascinating observations and experiences jammed into three hundred thirty-eight pages (paperback edition).

Erudite, sophisticated, and a longtime writer for the *New Yorker,* Gopnik chronicles the years he, his wife, and their young son spent living in the City of Light, where they moved because Gopnik and his wife wanted their son to be surrounded by beauty. Gopnik interweaves French history, culture, politics, and everyday life with illuminating personal stories. And if you like to laugh, pick up the book immediately and read the chapter "Barney in Paris," in which a Barney video finds its way into the family's suitcase, travels to Paris, and works its inexplicable spell on a gaggle of charming French children. The brief but illuminating chapter beautifully (and hilariously) encapsulates one of the memoir's governing ideas: Wherever you go, there you are.

Satori in Paris by Jack Kerouac

Everyone knows *On the Road*, right? But Kerouac also wrote other books, including this short memoir about nine days he spent in France searching for satori, meaning enlightenment, and his French heritage.

The Kerouac I found in this book comes off as an endearing, if lost, bumbler. It's the same rambling, intense, somewhat belligerent voice you might recall from his more commonly read works. He drinks a lot and gets into a lot of fights as he travels around France, but he is also charming and very, very funny.

The Statistical Probability of Love at First Sight by Jennifer E. Smith

I love airplanes, airports, and the idea of accidents that lead to unintended consequences, especially the good kind (remember the film *Sliding Doors*?). In addition to its concept, this young adult novel's great first line hooked me: *"There are so many ways it could have all turned out differently."*

The story begins in an airport where Hadley Sullivan has missed her flight to London, to which she is grudgingly traveling for her father's wedding. By missing her flight, Hadley meets London native Oliver, who is on his way home for a far more somber occasion. The two end up sitting next to each other on the flight and spend the whole night talking. Though it's largely a love story, the novel also integrates a significant subplot concerning Hadley's coming to terms with her father's new life and letting go of what can't be in favor of embracing what is. This is a lesson of which even adults sometimes need reminding.

Paris, My Sweet: A Year in the City of Light (and Dark Chocolate) by Amy Thomas

This is a fun memoir for foodies, especially if they happen to be sweet freaks, to enjoy on the beach or on a lazy Saturday. A sweets blogger living in New York, Thomas harbored a fascination for all things French. *Paris, My Sweet* covers the year she lived in Paris after being offered a sweet gig (I couldn't help myself) writing copy for Louis Vuitton.

Thomas addresses her acculturation process moving from one city to the other—making friends, getting around, learning the quirks of a new place—as well as what it means to find happiness in each city, with sweets serving as metaphors for her experiences. Each chapter covers a type of dessert or chocolate (macarons, cupcakes, tarts) that she discovers in Paris and a related one back in New York. Caution: May invite sweet cravings.

Madame Bovary's Daughter by Linda Urbach

Madame Bovary's Daughter picks up the story of Berthe, Emma Bovary's neglected, and ultimately orphaned, daughter from Gustav Flaubert's *Madame Bovary*. The story presents as a classic nineteenth-century coming-of-age saga with a twenty-first-century twist. The narrative follows Berthe's journey from being an orphan of twelve sent to live on a farm with her grandmother, to becoming a factory worker in the city of Lille then coming into her own as a young woman in Paris. Like a French female Tom Jones, Berthe experiences dramatic trials in her journey to achieve the life and love she seeks.

Urbach weaves plotlines into Berthe's story that also educate readers about nineteenth-century factory conditions and child labor, gender equality and the limits on women, providing a history lesson disguised as an adventure novel. Besides creating a conversation with historical realities of the age, Urbach enters into a sustained conversation with Flaubert's novel. Readers revisit familiar characters from Flaubert's classic, including the elder Madame Bovary (Berthe's grandmother), the pharmacist Homais and his family, the spinster laundress from the convent where Emma spent her early years, and Emma's former lover, the malevolent Rodolphe Boulanger. Emma also makes a few appearances through flashbacks, and Berthe exhibits personality traits that evoke both her parents as Flaubert created them.

Though some readers feel an aversion to contemporary books that build on classic novels, I find that they tend to spark my interest in the original. Urbach's absorbing take on Berthe sent me back to reread *Madame Bovary*.

Wild: From Lost to Found on the Pacific Crest Trail by Cheryl Strayed

At the age of twenty-six, having lost her mother, her marriage, and her equilibrium, Strayed embarked on a three-month solo hike along the Pacific Crest Trail. The experience is the subject of *Wild*, which climbed to the top of the *New York Times* bestseller list and was adapted into a feature film.

Of the memoir's over three hundred pages, many deal with one of my least favorite experiences: disappearing into heavily wooded nature, often in the vicinity of very high heights, for extended periods of time. Or what other people call camping. But Strayed's deep, beautiful, honest reflections drew me into her story. For example, when she found herself trying to figure out how to bear an entirely too heavy backpack before embarking on her hike, she was also at a moment in her life when she was trying to figure out *"how to bear the unbearable."* More than just drawing me in, her story inspired me, through its beauty, honesty, and deep insights, to think hard about my own journey through life.

CHAPTER 5

Novels in Letters and Multiple Perspectives

"Reading brings us unknown friends."

– Honoré de Balzac

When I told you about my childhood existential crisis in the introduction, I left out a crucial piece of the story: I did actually try to experience what it would be like to trade lives with someone. My plan wasn't especially radical or inventive. I convinced my best friend that we should change places for a day by trading clothes after our shared gymnastics class and going home with each other's mother. I convinced her despite the fact that she was a green-eyed blond as compared to brown-eyed, brunette me, and she was about three inches taller than I was. I even managed to be shocked and disappointed when our mothers failed to be fooled by my oh-so-cleverly crafted ruse.

With Plan A scuppered, Plan B involved reading loads and loads of books. Reading provided an outlet for my desire to experience someone else's inner life and to see the outer world through a fresh set of eyes (and *"I"s*), albeit vicariously. I've never lost my curiosity about others, but in recent years, I find myself gravitating towards novels that incorporate multiple perspectives (and thus eyes and *"I"s*) within a single story. These novels illuminate self and other in relationship, how tensions and misunderstandings arise, how personal preoccupations can lead to flawed perceptions, and perhaps how we might go about correcting misperceptions. The following ten novels do so through letter correspondences and other uses of multiple narrators that highlight relationships in their depth and complexity.

SALLY ALLEN

All the Light We Cannot See by Anthony Doerr

Doerr's elegant, lyrical prose and intricate characterization gives the reader so much beauty to linger over despite the emotionally heavy material of the setting: the lead-up to World War II in France and Germany and, later, occupied France and various battlefields in Europe and Russia.

Several storylines gradually move toward collision: a blind French girl, Marie-Laure, who flees with her father to the French coastal city of Saint-Malo; Werner, a German boy absorbed by the Nazi machine due to his talent for fixing radios; Reinhold von Rumpel, a rapacious German sergeant major hunting French treasures. Their stories take us into the most shadowy corners of the human animal with elegance and beauty.

This paradox preoccupied me as I read Doerr's novel: How can he write so beautifully about war, destruction, and evil? What does this signify? The dark phenomena the novel visits are not made beautiful through Doerr's writing; rather, their horror is cast into relief as juxtaposed with the beauty of the words and the acts of courage, goodness, and love that also rise up in the face of occupation and destruction.

Waves of emotion would wash over me at times while reading this novel, overwhelming me with grief at the human condition and how much suffering we cause one another. But it also made my heart balloon with hope for humanity because it showed me that even in the darkest times we have the capacity to seek the light, to survive and to thrive, to find beauty and meaning in the most unexpected places, and to push ourselves further than we ever thought possible in the name of love.

Where'd You Go, Bernadette by Maria Semple

Semple's at turns laugh-out-loud funny, moving, and bittersweet novel begins with what appear to be a random collection of correspondences—a report card, a school fundraising letter, emails the eponymous Bernadette exchanges with her India-based personal assistant and those exchanged between an obstreperous woman and a landscaper. The common thread among these communications emerges gradually: Eighth grade prodigy Bee, whose mother (Bernadette) has disappeared, is trying to piece together what happened to the once rising star architect.

As the story unfolds, and we travel from Seattle to California to the icy waters of Antarctica, a portrait emerges of a troubled woman, whose love for her daughter couldn't prevent her being undone by her personal demons. Mothers may have much to say about how Bernadette handles those demons and the impact on her bright, devoted daughter. But Semple also offers much to marvel at with her fresh and inventive narrative construction and whimsical, compassionate voice.

Boy, Snow, Bird by Helen Oyeyemi

Chock full of unexpected twists, Oyeyemi's novel is a retelling of *Snow White* set in mid-twentieth-century New England.

The eponymous Boy is a twenty-year-old girl when she flees her abusive father in New York circa 1953. She lands in Flax Hill, Massachusetts, where she meets and eventually marries the widowed Arturo Whitman, whose daughter Snow enchants everyone she meets, including Boy.

The happy idyll is broken after Boy gives birth to her own daughter, Bird, and a secret is revealed: The Whitmans are African Americans passing as white. Disturbed by how light-skinned Snow and dark-skinned Bird are compared to one another, Boy sends her light-skinned stepdaughter away to live with Arturo's sister, Clara, banished by her family because she was too dark to pass. Boy's decision—indefensible but born of fierce maternal overprotectiveness—has far-reaching repercussion on both girls in this charged, powerful, and lyrical examination of race and conceptions of beauty, and their perils, in which Boy, Snow, and Bird each have a turn narrating their stories.

The Husband's Secret by **Liane Moriarty**

Australian author Moriarty explores the dramas of suburban family life with at times cringe-worthy acuity. In *The Husband's Secret*, devoted wife, mother, and Tupperware saleswoman Cecilia Fitzpatrick finds a letter that harbors a secret her husband means to keep hidden until after his death. Pulled into the story is advertising executive Tess O'Leary, whose son attends the same school as Cecilia's children, where the secretary is Rachel Crowley, whose teenaged daughter was murdered decades earlier.

The three narratives move, in excruciatingly perfect pacing, toward an explosive collision. Through the lens of each woman, readers are invited to consider how far they would go to protect the ones they love and, with slightly more sinister undertones, how far they would go to protect the lives they're living. Plot twists and turns come in spades, along with moral quandaries. Perhaps most intriguing, and discussion provoking, is the way Moriarty imagines how characters's lives might have turned out had circumstances been different.

2 A.M. at the Cat's Pajamas
by Marie-Helene Bertino

This novel follows multiple characters as they traverse the city of Philadelphia over the course of one day, beginning in the early hours of the day before Christmas Eve. As snow flurries descend on the city, Mrs. Rose Santiago clears her stoop. Nearby, aspiring jazz singer Madeleine Altimari, two days from her tenth birthday, smokes her late mother's Newport Menthols and practices her vocals in her dissolute and disengaged father's apartment. In another part of the city, Jack Lorca prepares to open his club, the Cat's Pajamas. But an impromptu visit from the police leads to Jack receiving a five-figure fine and promises that any more violations will result in his club being closed. Meanwhile, he has promised his teenaged son Alex, an aspiring guitarist headed down a dangerous path, a shot at performing with the house band.

Other adventurers inhabiting various corners of the city include Sarina, Madeline's fifth grade teacher; Ben, Sarina's prom date of twenty years ago; Pedro, Mrs. Santiago's peripatetic dog; Ted Stempel and his pit bull puppy, Malcolm; and Madeline's classmates Clare Kelly and Jill McCormick. As the day ticks by minute by minute, hour by hour, their lives intersect in ways ridiculous and profound through a narrative that takes us into the consciousness of multiple characters. Yet this shifting of perspectives is so fluid that it is as if we are ghosts gliding through walls. We see the larger landscape, and we see the fine details.

One of the hallmarks of great writing lies in an author's ability to recast familiar experiences and emotional truths, and at this, Bertino excels in particular. Several times, I came across a description that inspired me to stop, think, and admire, notably: *"She could sneak in there, but she must be quiet, like cancer"* and *"Sarina's cheeks turn the color of ham."*

The Night Circus by Erin Morgenstern

While a superstorm was rattling my windowpanes (and dropping a tree in my yard), I got lost in this marvel of a novel. It is indeed about a circus that is only open at night. Le Cirque des Rêves, as it is called, provides the site for a competition between two magicians, Celia and Marco, that spans decades.

The details of the battle, including how the winner is determined and what happens to the loser, are shrouded in mystery. The emerging specifics, revealed as the novel weaves back and forth through time and points of view, pit Celia and Marco in battle not only with each other but with the very magicians who trained them.

Intricately plotted and saturated with dreamlike settings, mysterious events, and mesmerizing characters, this magical, utterly absorbing read is evocative, dark, and shadowy, like its beautiful cover.

You Knew Me When by Emily Lieber

In Liebert's debut novel, Katherine Hill's non-stop schedule as a high-powered cosmetics company executive doesn't leave her much time to reflect on her past. That is, until she is named in the will of an old family friend and mentor, Luella. Returning to her hometown in Vermont, Katherine faces the life (and people) she left behind, including her one-time best friend Laney. As close as sisters growing up, their paths diverged with bitterness and acrimony post-college. Luella has left the two women her house and possessions, forcing them to collaborate on one last project together, in hopes that the two women will learn to forgive each other.

I found this novel difficult to put down owing to both the story and the narrative structure. The novel moves back and forth in time, from the present (narrated in the third person from both women's points of view) to the past (narrated in the first person from both girls's points of view). Handled with finesse, this back and forth offers dual perspectives—we see the girls as they see themselves but also how those selves exist in their larger worlds. It also allows us to understand the forces that shaped the girls in childhood, their character strengths and flaws, and how those play out in adulthood. It's a very human portrait of a friendship that went off the rails, and the struggle to get past old wounds.

The Lowland by Jhumpa Lahiri

Lahiri's novel follows the divergent fates of two brothers, Subhash and Udayan, born in Calcutta at the dawn of India's independence. As children, the boys were as close as two siblings could be, but as the years progress, their paths take them in separate directions. Subhash travels to the U.S. to study while Udayan stays in Calcutta and joins a political rebellion.

Lahiri's narrative shifts points of view, weaving from past to present and back again, and dialogue is not set off in quotation marks or otherwise demarcated with speech indicators. The cumulative effects of this storytelling provoke in the reader a sense of dislocation, echoing that experienced by the brothers, who cannot bend the world, internal or external, to meet their will. The novel invites the reader to ponder how deeply we can claim access to the inner lives of others—their most closely guarded desires, fears, and transgressions.

Little Children by Tom Perrotta

Perrotta's novels are known for their spirited and often hilarious explorations of suburban life. *Little Children* isn't his most recent, but it is perhaps his darkest (and some might say best).

Sarah has grown weary of her older husband Richard and embarks on a passionate affair with Tom, the "prom king" househusband of filmmaker Kathy. Against the backdrop of these suburban intrigues, another narrative plays out. Sexual predator Ronnie McGorvey moves in with his widowed mother May, inviting vengeful protests from concerned neighbors, fueled by his being a suspect in the unsolved disappearance of a child. Delving deeply into Ronnie's psyche, Perrotta achieves the near impossible: He invites readers to sympathize with a lonely, deeply troubled soul who may or may not have committed a heinous crime. Though often funny, the novel also highlights the tricky, flawed nature of individual perception.

The Imperfectionists by Tom Rachman

The main "character" in this novel is actually a thing—an English-language newspaper in Rome facing its dying days. Each chapter, which could stand alone as a short story, follows one person connected to the paper. Reporters, owners, copywriters, stringers, even readers (and more) are revealed in overlapping stories that are at turns tragic, comic, and heartbreaking.

Deeply affecting, the novel provides a deep study of a newspaper and the newspaper industry and crafts a portrait of an age and a way of life as they slip into oblivion. Rachman's sensitively rendered characters will make readers wonder about what we do and do not know about the people whose lives intersect with ours on a daily basis.

CHAPTER 6

Novels About Connection, Community, and Family

"Reading is that fruitful miracle of a communication in the midst of solitude."

— Marcel Proust

In addition to providing exposure to worlds beyond my own, books are where I learned and continue to learn about myself, and especially how to communicate and connect. When I feel uncertain or overwhelmed by either of the latter two, I turn to books. I suspect this is what compelled me to pull out a book and begin reading in the middle of my friend's eighth birthday party … until her mother told me she could have my mom pick me up. I put the book away then in favor of joining the birthday revelries. And I've learned, in adulthood, not to turn to books for insight into how to communicate and connect while actually *at* a party.

These desires for communication and connection lie at the heart of the modern age's groundbreaking inventions, including the printing press, the telephone, the airplane, the Internet. The printing press and the Internet, invented centuries apart, both enabled broader participation in local and global conversations. The telephone and the airplane shrank our conceptions of physical distance. These inventions reflect back at us our desire to be seen and heard, to be part of something larger, more potent than our isolated selves. Though it may brush up against a desire to be exceptional, to stand out, to be an "individual," the desire to connect can inspire us, in the best of times, to set aside self-interest and see ourselves as part of a larger whole. These ten books provide answers to the question, "What does it mean to connect?" as characters struggle, in the shadow of betrayal, loss, and tragic legacies, to move forward, find redemption, and nurture connection, community, and family, whether by blood or by choice.

A Working Theory of Love by Scott Hutchins

Recently divorced thirty-something Neill is working on a project to create a sentient computer. The catch? The computer is constructed largely around the journals of his father, who committed suicide. Alongside the race to complete the computer runs Neill's romantic quests. He meets twenty-one-year-old Rachel, a student who belongs to a cult, Pure Encounters, whose purpose is reconnecting human experience to the body.

What does it mean to be human in the digital age? This seems to be the fundamental question the novel explores, both through Neill's computer work and his romantic relationships. They suggest that love, intangible, ineffable, and defying explanation, can offer no guarantees, but it's the only thing truly worth pursuing.

The Girl Who Chased the Moon by Sarah Addison Allen

Allen (no relation) has earned a following with her gentle novels that explore family, community, and love, with a dollop of something otherworldly added to the mix. I save them for when I'm feeling blue because they always cheer me up.

The Girl Who Chased the Moon tells the intertwined stories of Emily Benedict and Julia Winterson. After her mother's death, teenaged Emily shows up on her grandfather's doorstep in the Southern town where her mother grew up. Her grandfather is a stranger to her, and the two struggle to connect. Another disconnect is revealed in Emily's new home, between the mother she knew and the woman the town remembers— or rather, who they wish to forget. Like Emily, Julia is also nursing emotional wounds. She returned to town after a long absence to take over her father's restaurant and bakes cakes that have an almost healing ability. As their stories begin to overlap, the question becomes whether Julia can also heal herself.

The Invention of Hugo Cabret by Brian Selznick

Though classified as a middle-grade reader, Selznick's uplifting story about finding connection and purpose has resonated with readers of all ages. Set in Paris between the two World Wars, the book introduces us to twelve-year-old Hugo, whose father has died suddenly. Hugo lives inside a train station's walls with his dissolute Uncle Claude, whose job is to maintain the station's clockwork. Except Claude has vanished, leaving Hugo to survive by his wits, pilfering necessities from various carts and hiding from the station master.

Hugo's only companion is a broken automaton. When he's not tending to the clocks, Hugo focuses on trying to repair the automaton, a project begun by his father. This particular automaton has a special feature: When functioning, it writes. If only Hugo can fix it, he believes, it will communicate a message from his father. Hugo conspires to steal the gears needed to repair the automaton from a toy stall in the station manned by Georges Méliès, based on the actual turn-of-the-century French cinema legend. The onetime revolutionary filmmaker lost everything around World War I and is left, in his waning years, with a train station toyshop to provide his livelihood. Their lives intersect in unexpected ways, drawing in other characters, including Isabelle, an orphan who lives with Méliès and his wife and who is also marked by loss.

The book's unique feature is in how the story unfolds: Selznick tells some parts through words and others through black and white drawings and images from Méliès's films. The illustrations move the narrative forward and allow readers to experience visually moments of tension, suspense, anxiety, passion, and contentment that, in real life, often feel bigger than words can contain. This powerful visual component may be one significant reason the novel adapted so seamlessly to the screen as Hugo, directed by Martin Scorsese. Having read the book and seen the film within a month of each other, I was enchanted by both equally, a rare occurrence for me.

The essence of the story is beautifully encapsulated in a scene that appears in both the book and the movie: Hugo and Isabelle stand looking out a clockwork window. Isabelle has

SALLY ALLEN

just been worrying about what her purpose is. *I like to imagine that the world is one big machine,"* Hugo tells her as they gaze at the city beyond. *"You know, machines never have any extra parts. They have the exact number and type of parts they need. So I figure if the entire world is a big machine, I have to be here for some reason. And that means you have to be here for some reason, too."* Whether it's from a twelve-year-old boy at the beginning of his life or a senior confronting the final chapters in his story, *The Invention of Hugo Cabret* shows us how a sense of purpose connects us in the present and provides hope for the future.

The Vacationers by Emma Straub

This novel revolves around a family in crisis as they embark on a two-week vacation to Mallorca that was intended to celebrate Jim and Franny's thirty-fifth wedding anniversary. But Jim has lost his job at a magazine, let go for an offense that is only revealed halfway through the novel by his wife Franny, a journalist with an extravagant spirit. Their daughter Sylvia has just graduated high school and has her own agenda for the vacation, while son Bobby brings his much older girlfriend Carmen, who none of the family likes. Rounding out the group are Franny's best friend Charles and his husband Lawrence.

I wouldn't call it a plot-driven novel, though stuff does happen—a few dramas, a few wishes fulfilled, and much food consumed, often prepared by Franny. What makes the novel compulsively readable is Straub's success in making the reader care about her characters's inner lives and the dynamics among them. She moves in and out of the consciousness of each player, often hitting on emotional truths with wit and pathos. It's also a novel whose characters have strong opinions—about younger men and older women, about marriage and parenthood, and, happily enough, about reading as a presence in our lives.

The Museum of Extraordinary Things by Alice Hoffman

With its elegant prose and mysterious story, *The Museum of Extraordinary Things* mesmerized me. Set in New York City at the turn of the twentieth century, the novel, narrated in first and third person, follows Coralie and Eddie, whose tales are told in alternating chapters, as they circle around and toward each other.

First, we meet Coralie Sardie, who stars as a mermaid in a museum of oddities run by her father, the "Professor." While on a mission for him, Coralie encounters Eddie Cohen. Eddie has abandoned his Orthodox community and father, first to run errands that lead him into a debauched underworld and then to become a photographer. Though drawn to him, Coralie returns to her life in Brooklyn without making contact with Eddie. He returns to his work in Manhattan, which includes capturing the devastating aftermath of the infamous Triangle Shirtwaist Factory fire. The tragedy brings simmering conflicts between the city's disparate classes into relief and entangles Eddie in the case of a missing woman, about whom

Coralie may know something.

Hoffman also crafts a significant character of the city it-self, with its (figurative and literal) dark alleys and moments of beauty, providing a richly conjured map of a lost place and time. The narrative inspires readers to reflect on how much and how little have changed about both the city and the human condition, and provides a reminder that pleasure and beauty, though often conflated, are quite different experiences.

The Light Between Oceans by M. L. Stedman

Stedman's gripping novel explores the ramifications of one woman's desperate longing to become a mother. In the wake of World War I, vivacious Isabelle and stoic Tom, a principled veteran, fall in love and move to a remote island in Western Australia, where Tom will serve as lighthouse keeper. The two set up house and their own secluded but cheery world.

Their island idyll begins to fall apart as Isabelle suffers two miscarriages and a stillbirth. The latter is followed, from Isabelle's perspective, by a miracle: A small boat washes ashore carrying a baby and a lifeless man. Protocol dictates Tom record and report the incident. But Isabelle persuades him to grant her one day with the baby, which quickly turns into more as Tom cannot bear to aggrieve his wife. In their isolation, Tom and Isabelle dispel thoughts that the baby's mother may be alive and mourning the loss of her child. What happens next in Stedman's nuanced story invites us to consider how far we would go to realize our desires.

This is Where I Leave You by **Jonathan Tropper**

The page-turner of a novel follows Judd Foxman after his marriage implodes (he walks in on his wife and boss *in flagrante delicto*) and his father has died. His father's request was for his wife (a therapist) and four children to sit shiva for him—in Jewish tradition, seven days of mourning during which family members receive visitors wishing to pay their respects. Besides Judd, there are Wendy (who is married to Barry, the stereotypical hedge fund guy), Paul (who runs the family business and is struggling to conceive with his wife, Alice), and Phillip (the youngest and the family screw-up).

Old wounds resurface and rivalries resume over the seven days, along with quite a few revelations. Consider yourself warned: Tropper's punchy sentences, witty dialogue, and inflammatory family dynamics reach up out of the book and grab the reader by the (figurative) lapels, making it almost impossible to put down.

We Are All Completely Beside Ourselves by **Karen Joy Fowler**

Beginning "in the middle," Rosemary Cooke narrates her family's story, which includes a fugitive brother, a lost sister, and an explosive secret. The writing is witty and engaging from the beginning, and I had little idea where this quirky, loquacious storyteller was taking me until the identity of Rosemary's sister, and how she was lost, are revealed late in the novel.

Propelling us through this mystery is a madcap plot and bitingly funny prose. But the novel's underlying story meditates on serious questions about how our early sibling relationships, and the narratives we construct around them, shape our mannerisms and characters. More significantly, they can become the yardstick against which we measure our individual selves.

The Good Luck of Right Now by **Matthew Quick**

Pushing forty, Bartholomew Neil is socially maladapted, beset by crippling self-doubts, and achingly lost. His mother, with whom Bartholomew lived and who he nursed during a long illness, has recently died, forcing him to take charge of his life for the first time. His journey to this new life is recounted in letters Bartholomew writes to his mother's favorite movie star: Richard Gere.

During his literal and figurative travels, Bartholomew draws in a group of eclectic companions, including a librarian with a devastating past, her brother, and a defrocked priest. But his mother and the lessons she bestowed on him are never far from his thoughts, as he struggles to hold on to her greatest gift: faith in the eponymous *"good luck of right now,"* insistently choosing to look for the positive in every situation. An equal parts heartbreaking and heartwarming story about learning to move past trauma and create your own community, the novel also serves to remind us that the lessons we learn in childhood stay with and transform us, even as we go on to create our own adult lives and families.

Lucky Us by Amy Bloom

The first two sentences start with a bang: *"My father's wife died. My mother said we should drive down to his place and see what might be in it for us."* The first person narrator here is twelve-year-old Eva, whose mother leaves her with the newly widowed Edgar and his sixteen-year-old daughter Iris and takes off. Without much preamble, at least of the narrative sort, the half-sisters seem to bond, and when Iris decides to leave Ohio and head to Hollywood intent on film stardom, Eva joins her.

Did you notice how I slipped in that bit about how the girls were from Ohio? This is my clumsy approximation of how Bloom socks the reader with surprising revelations, both about her characters and what happens to them. It's a story that leaps from one point of view to the next, from one place to the next, often without prelude. In addition to Eva's first person narrative, the story unfolds through third person limited omniscient and letters among the characters. But gaps and holes serve a purpose, as do rests in a musical score or empty space on a canvas—as inextricable counterpoint to the action or subject. In this sense, these gaps mimic how we experience life in the moment, doing the best we can despite incomplete understanding.

This is partly why I don't want to tell you too much about the plot. I'm itching to, but no. This is a novel to jump into blind, and trust. A few things it won't hurt to know: This isn't a war story; though it takes place in the shadow of World War II, the war is more background than foreground. It's a book about creating your self and your family and finding your way in a world that can be unforgiving but still beautiful and redemptive.

UNLOCKING WORLDS

CHAPTER 7

Novels About the
American Experience

*"How many a man has dated a new era
in his life from the reading of a book."*

– Henry David Thoreau

When I was a little girl, I lived for the summers when I traded my home in New York City for my maternal grandmother's house on a Greek island so tiny it rarely appears on maps. As it has no airport, the island is only reachable by boat. During my childhood, our luggage would then be transported from the ferry to my grandmother's house by donkey. Her four-room house had electricity, a stove, a refrigerator, one bathroom, running water, and one telephone, centrally located in the hallway that connected the four rooms. These constituted the sum total of modern conveniences. Visiting my grandmother felt like being transported back through time to my mother's childhood, a world away from my bustling, frantic, regular life in New York. My family and I were the only Americans on the island, and though our ethnicity is Greek, my siblings and I were "the little Americans."

This experience shuttling back and forth between old world and new awakened in me, from a very young age, a consciousness of "America" as not only physical place but as a state of mind and an idea, one that is continually evolving. I understood that being American was not about bloodlines or a singular history, or set traditions and beliefs. Instead, being American was about coexisting, too often uneasily, among diverse histories, traditions, and beliefs—those who came to America seeking "a better life" (the narrative of my family), those who were brought against their will and subjugated, those whose way of life was wiped out. For better and worse, these are all part of the American experience, captured never more eloquently, for me, than by James Baldwin when he wrote, *"American history is longer, larger, more various, more beautiful, and more terrible than anything anyone has ever said about it."* The following ten books, though far from definitive of the American experience, capture various, beautiful, and terrible American experiences.

The Good Lord Bird by James McBride

McBride's National Book Award-winning novel reconstructs the life of John Brown in the years before and through his ill-fated 1859 raid on Harper's Ferry. The narrator is Henry Shackleford, a young slave whom Brown kidnaps/rescues. Henry's playful irreverence is revealed from the first two lines and holds up to the very last page of this novel, remarkable for its capacity to make us laugh out loud as we're shedding bitter tears: *"I was born a colored man and don't you forget it. But I lived as a colored woman for seventeen years."*

Henry lives with his father in Kansas Territory, where Brown arrives with his followers. After a shoot-out, Henry's father winds up dead, and Brown takes off with Henry. But because of the sack he was wearing, Henry is mistaken for a girl and, after eating a large onion, christened "Onion" by Brown. Since Brown doesn't stop talking and preaching long enough for Onion to explain the misunderstanding, he keeps up the charade as a she and follows Brown, often reluctantly, through his (mis)adventures in Kansas and through the raid on Harper's Ferry.

Reading this novel, I kept thinking of the British expression, "What are you playing at?" What *is* McBride playing at in this novel, in which just about everyone is ridiculous? John Brown comes off as a somewhat deranged lunatic with explosive diarrhea of the mouth. An effete Frederick Douglas has two wives but still tries to score with Onion. A good number of Brown's followers appear to be half-wits and fond of the drink. The only character with any gravitas is Harriet Tubman. And yet, we get a sense that McBride's caricatures, while irreverent, aren't derisive. He makes clear that no matter how crazy or ridiculous Brown and his followers may have been, there was still only one right side, and they were on it.

McBride's highly entertaining book—and therefore challenging, because it is an entertaining book about slavery—reveals the complexity of humanity and pushes us to ask tough questions: Are good and bad the same as right and wrong? Is it possible that you can do bad things and still have redeemable qualities, or that you can do great things and still be human and flawed? McBride gives us a way to talk about the past that offers humor as a way of healing. In an interview with *Guernica Magazine*, he explained, *"Some things are so terrible that you just have to laugh at them ... It releases some of the pain from the shotgun wound."*

Ethan Frome by Edith Wharton

This novel of repressed passion and its ensuing tragedy (this isn't really a spoiler because … *Edith Wharton*) should probably come with a warning label: May be harmful for the existentially depressed. Wharton's brilliant prose does provide a foil against the darkness of the story, and she excels at revealing character through spare but pointedly crafted details, gestures, dialogue, and scene.

The eponymous Ethan Frome falls for his sickly wife's pretty young cousin, the orphaned and displaced Mattie, who hails from Connecticut. Mattie moves into the couple's Massachusetts home to help care for Ethan's wife, Zeena, whose pastimes include curling up by the fire to read books about the digestive system, traveling around Massachusetts to visit medical specialists, leveling acidic barbs at Ethan and Mattie, and plotting to make everyone around her as miserable as she is.

During a bleak Massachusetts winter in the town of Starkfield (named with Dickensian flair, yes?) that provides copious opportunities to reflect mood through descriptions of the weather, Ethan and Mattie's mutual attraction grows, like a plant in a too-small pot. With nowhere to go and no hope of being consummated in their repressive New England society, their love implodes. The ending is ironic tragedy times a million billions.

Passing by Nella Larson

It was while reading *The Great Gatsby* for my local library's One Book, One Town program that *Passing*, which I first read in graduate school and which also takes place in New York during the 1920s, called me back. Set in Harlem, the story revolves around the reunion between two women, Clare Kendry and Irene Redfield, both of mixed-race ancestry, who grew up together. Their paths diverged in childhood after Clare's white father died, and she went to live with his two sisters. In adulthood, Irene, from whose point of view the story is told, marries a black doctor and is an active participant in the black community, including serving on the Negro Welfare League (NWL) committee.

On a trip to Chicago, Irene runs into Clare at a hotel and discovers that Clare is "passing" as a white woman: Clare's white husband, Jack Bellew, doesn't know that Clare is biracial. Years later in Harlem, Clare seeks a relationship with a reluctant Irene and won't take no for an answer, visiting Irene at home, attending a NWL dance, and socializing publicly. At a lunch with Clare and another biracial friend, Irene meets Jack, who assumes all the women present at the lunch are white and goes on a racist diatribe that causes Irene to consider the risks Clare is taking, especially in a time riddled with tremendous anxiety about "the color line." Clare, whose motives are never quite clear, either to Irene or to the reader, appears unconcerned. But her excursions build to a tragic climax in this difficult and important novel that confronts the anguish and rage caused by racism.

The Buddha in the Attic by Julie Otsuka

The novel tells the stories of Japanese "picture brides" shipped to California during the first decades of the twentieth century to marry men they knew only from their photos, which were often as inaccurate as the men's claims of financial success. Narrated in prose that blooms poetically and musically, the writing's rhythm compels the reader (certainly this reader) to follow the story to its conclusion, preferably in one sitting.

I haven't mentioned that it's narrated in the first person plural, the collective "we," potentially referencing any and all Japanese women who came to the U.S. at that time. In this sense, the novel is panoramic in scope, though it's a slim one hundred twenty-nine pages (paperback edition). Michael Upchurch, writing for *The Seattle Times*, aptly compared it to a pointillist painting, *"composed of bright spots of color; vignettes that bring whole lives to light in a line or two, adding up to a vibrant group portrait."* How Otsuka manages this is nothing short of a technical marvel, and here is why: Typically, historical fiction succeeds and appeals when it enables identification between then and now, between the narrator and the reader, between the familiar and the strange. But *The Buddha in the Attic* never quite closes the gap between reader and subject (until the last chapter) and doesn't particularly seem to want to. Perhaps we're never meant to identify with Otsuka's "we" as much as we're meant to have our minds opened to what it would be like to step into a world turned upside down with no way out. Otsuka accomplished this extraordinarily well without ever losing me as a reader.

Harvard Square by André Aciman

Aciman's unnamed narrator is (like the author) from a Jewish Egyptian family and is working towards his Ph.D. at Harvard. When the novel opens, he has failed his oral exams and is in danger of being expelled. During the summer before his second attempt to pass his orals, the narrator meets Kalaj, nicknamed Kalashnikov for his combative language and behavior. The Tunisian Muslim taxi driver is potentially facing deportation and is both drawn to and repelled by American culture, depending on the progress of his case. The narrator also exists in the margins, on the brink of either full membership in the intellectual and (by extension) cultural world to which he seeks entry or irrevocable expulsion from it. In this sense, he both identifies with Kalaj and resists identifying with him. Their bond deepens, along with their animosity, as they move through the summer toward their separate outcomes.

This mesmerizing novel was impossible to put down owing largely to two things: The poetic, rhythmic quality of Aciman's prose (the rhythms shift in accordance with the narrator's emotional temperament) and his razor-sharp insights into the human psyche and the immigrant experience.

Shopgirl by Steve Martin

In Martin's novella (perfect when you want to read one book straight through), an omniscient narrator with a strong presence, a sharp eye for detail, and a great sense of the absurd tells the intersecting stories of three Los Angeles residents. Mirabelle is a twenty-six year-old artist and Vermont transplant who spends her days working in Neiman Marcus's glove department. There, she meets Ray, wealthy, divorced, and fifty years old, who showers attention and gifts on her, though he has no long-term intentions for their relationship. Meanwhile, Mirabelle's erstwhile boyfriend Jeremy, who is slightly younger than she, seems to lack direction, until he stumbles into an unexpected career opportunity.

The narrative voice proceeds with an almost clinical remove from the characters yet devotes such careful attention to their inner lives that they feel whole, real, and fully developed. Funny and sweet, the book manages to be hopeful about the American ideal of reinvention and creating the life we want without being saccharine.

The Goldfinch by Donna Tartt

Tartt's Pulitzer Prize winning novel is one of those books I find most difficult to write about: To reduce it is impossible, and I fear attempting to unwrap its mysteries will somehow dim its magic. The act of trying to reminds me of dissecting frogs in ninth grade Biology. They were so much more enjoyable to behold while frolicking through the grass than when splayed out and stuck with pins to hold their formaldehyde-soaked bodies into place.

The novel tells the story of Theo Decker, who is thirteen years old when he loses his mother in a terrorist attack at a New York art museum. Along with his life, Theo walks away with a priceless painting, Carel Fabritius's enigmatic *Goldfinch*, a favorite of his mother's. We follow Theo—from Park Avenue (where he stays with a school friend's distant, patrician family) to Las Vegas (where his dissolute father takes him) back to New York (where he finds a home with a surprising acquaintance)—as he searches for connection, meaning, and hope.

In Tartt's capable hands, Theo's singular journey is transformed into a sweeping epic with implications for us all, and Tartt's extravagant details, unforgettable characters and compassionate portrayal of them have prompted deserved comparisons with Charles Dickens. Like Dickens's Pip, Theo makes many bad choices and takes many missteps, but Tartt's richly imagined portrait of his world makes it impossible for readers not to root for Theo to find what he is seeking. Underlying his personal journey of reinvention is a larger message about the power of community, love, and art to sustain and inspire us.

The Beginning of Everything by Robin Schneider

This young adult novel hooked me with its first thought-provoking paragraph: *"Sometimes I think that everyone has a tragedy waiting for them, that the people buying milk in their pajamas or picking their noses at stoplights could be only moments away from disaster. That everyone's life, no matter how unre-markable, has a moment when it will become extraordinary—a single encounter after which everything that really matters will happen."*

The story takes place during the narrator, Ezra Faulkner's, senior year of high school. Ezra's "personal tragedy" happens at the end of his junior year: He's in a car accident that ends his tennis career. Though he didn't have professional aspirations, being a star tennis player was his defining activity at school. It was, he believed, his ticket to the "cool kid" lunch table and would later get him into college. In the wake of the accident, Ezra has to re-imagine himself, who he wants to be, and where he wants to belong. These issues are what make his story so relatable, because we never really stop having to recalibrate ourselves in life.

The Beginning of Everything is also a book lover's book, with literary references galore (including some esoteric ones to theorist Michel Foucault). When the story begins, Ezra is reading *The Great Gatsby*, and that novel's central themes and ideas figure prominently in Schneider's book, echoing in her characterizations and use of language. The narrative voice is earnest, questioning, caring, and hopeful (because tragedy, in this conception, leads to things mattering). Ezra's struggle to reinvent himself invites us to appreciate how every day that we choose to get up, get dressed, and get going takes a leap of faith.

This Beautiful Life by Helen Shulman

In Shulman's unsettling (in an important way) novel, fifteen-year-old Jake Bergamot makes a bad decision with far-reaching consequences. An unsolicited, sexually explicit video arrives in his in-box from thirteen-year-old Daisy Cavanaugh, and Jake forwards it to a friend, who then forwards it to four friends and so on until the video has gone viral. The book explores the ramifications—legal, moral, familial—of one thoughtless action whose impact reverberates into ever widening circles.

We are raising our children in an age when privacy is gradually eroding, like a coastline disappearing by inches with each passing year. For parents like me, who grew up at a time when privacy did exist, when it was possible to make and learn from mistakes in a relatively circumscribed environment, Shulman's novel brings up disquieting questions about the consequences of everything being documented and nothing disappearing, especially in an increasingly litigious America.

The Absolutely True Story of a Part-Time Indian by Sherman Alexie

When I come across articles in which critics shame adults for reading young adult literature because it's purportedly not complicated, I find myself wondering whether these critics have read Alexie's remarkable autobiographical novel. It tells the story of fourteen-year-old Arnold Spirit, nicknamed

Junior, a budding cartoonist, frequent target of bullies, and resident of the Spokane Indian Reservation. Early in the novel, Junior comes to a painful decision: He cannot become the person that he wants to be if he remains on the Reservation. This decision leads him to withdraw from the Reservation's high school in favor of attending one in a wealthy, white neighborhood.

With equal parts humor and heartbreak, Junior describes his deeply loving and supportive but also troubled family, and the alcoholism and violence that surround him on the Reservation. Without judging, he acknowledges what *is* while also recognizing that the causes are complicated. His decision to leave the Reservation's high school causes outrage in his community, including from Rowdy, his best friend and protector. Though his family and a few close friends do support him, Junior struggles with his choice, both emotionally and practically. Getting from the Reservation to his new school often requires walking long distances as he does not have a car or money for public transportation. At first, he's ostracized and bullied at his new school. But Junior is determined to turn his enemies and critics into friends, or at least not enemies, and more importantly to choose the life he wants.

His resilience, refusal to fail, and refusal to accept the categories others try to put him in are both humbling and uplifting. The novel makes us contemplate the dark chapters of our nation's history that can never be made right. But it also explores a broader question at the heart of the American experience: How do we move forward in a way that honors the past, acknowledges that any choice is an imperfect choice, and allows us to choose life, even in the midst of mourning?

CHAPTER 8

Novels About What Happens When Things Fall Apart

"To acquire the habit of reading is to construct for yourself a refuge from almost all the miseries of life."

– W. Somerset Maugham

I t hurts when our ideals fail to live up to our expectations. We witness this crashing down across human history and, more personally, across the landscape of our individual lives. My first profound experience of loss was not so much the loss of an ideal as of an idyll, and idol: When I was twelve, my maternal grandmother died of cancer. So many of my happiest childhood memories were spent with her during my summers in Greece, and in the winter, she lived with my family in New York. She would arrive in the fall, and I would look forward to the day we would pick her up at the airport like it was Christmas morning. In the arrivals area at my mother's side, I would peer anxiously at the glass doors waiting to see her black-clad figure emerge. Airports still carry this nostalgic association for me, and I rarely pass through a customs line without thinking of her. The grief at having her ripped from my life felt insurmountable. I could not conceive of a long future stretching before me without my grandmother there to share in it. During this time, reading became curative for me. It wasn't just a refuge, a chance to lose myself in someone else's world; it also provided answers. Though I would not have been able to articulate it in this way at that time, I was grappling with the suffering that comes from confronting our helplessness in the face of mortality. I needed to understand how to move forward, to hold onto hope for the future.

Sara Crewe from *A Little Princess* was my first literary model for how to wrestle with loss and still maintain faith that life can be beautiful, even if it's not exactly the life hoped for or imagined. And books continue to show me how to carry on in the face of life's inevitable heartbreaks. Any number of novels I read could fit into this category. The ones I've chosen for this section are those that have, at their center, a fundamental breakdown, whether it's of a relationship or family, of the social and/or political order, or even of something as fundamental as our governing notion of time as linear. Though the breakdowns each story dramatizes vary considerably in scale, from single relationships to world orders, what the stories all share is the struggle to carry on in the face of a foundational collapse.

The Time Traveler's Wife by Audrey Niffenegger

In this hauntingly beautiful debut novel, Henry suffers from a genetic disorder that causes him to travel through time spontaneously, without being able to control where and when he goes. He falls in love with artist Clare, and the novel, narrated in alternating first-person perspectives, follows the progress of their relationship. Though this is (like the novels in Chapter Three) a time travel novel, the heart of the story is how Henry and Clare wrestle with the limitations posed by his disorder and how it affects their relationship.

One significant way his disorder challenges their relationship is that it doesn't progress in a linear fashion: Henry pops in and out of Clare's life at different times and ages in ways that push the limits of comprehension, and tear at the heart. As with any time travel story, the willingness to suspend

92

disbelief is required, but the reader is rewarded for taking the leap into Niffenegger's cohesive, heartbreaking world. In stunning prose, she renders a story of love that endures, and thrives, in the most challenging conditions.

The Affair by Colette Freedman

At times gripping but also infuriating, Freedman's novel explores a marriage collapsing under the strain of a husband's affair with a younger woman. Kathy is the wife of eighteen years, mother to Robert's two teenaged daughters, partner in his film production business, and homemaker. Stephanie is the attractive, driven, career woman, who increasingly pressures Robert to make a decision about his future with her, which means leaving his wife. And Robert? He likes to have his cake, and he also likes to have his ice cream, if you know what I mean.

Though told in alternating chapters from each character's point of view (in third person limited omniscient), Robert emerges as, by far, the least sympathetic of the three, primarily because he creates an elaborate, though fragile, reality to justify his relationship with Stephanie. Convinced by Robert that his marriage is long dead, Stephanie pushes him to end it. Kathy, however, is devastated to discover that the life she has built is in shambles. Frankly, you might wonder why she doesn't kick him to the curb. It's a fascinating read that had me flipping the pages late into the night to see how events would play out, but it might not be the best book to read when you're feeling depressed about men.

Fahrenheit 451 by Ray Bradbury

A high school reading list staple, Bradbury's dystopian classic follows the transformation of Guy Montag, a "fireman" of the future. His job is to gather and burn books; their existence is seen as a threat to the security of the state and the peace of mind of its citizens. On one of his missions, Guy encounters a woman who chooses to burn with her books rather than leave them behind, and the experience leaves him shaken. An awakening, both of curiosity and questioning, begins taking shape in Guy and leads him down a difficult but ultimately creative path. The allegorical plot is, on one very important level, about books. But it's also about ambiguity and complexity, and the very good reasons why we both fear and need them.

Rereading *Fahrenheit 451* in one burst proved difficult for me, largely because the pace and structure of the sentences possess the qualities of a nightmare, with stops and starts, fragments and grotesque imagery. It was written in 1953 but prophesied the constant noise and filler of our contemporary world, along with the isolation and loneliness that virtual connection and communication invite. It predicts us in other ways that should alarm us as well: our obsessions with speed, convenience, and disposability. Not an easy novel to read or reread, it is well worth the effort as its themes and message are deeply relevant for our time.

The Lifeboat by Charlotte Rogan

In 1914, the world is on the edge of war, and an ocean-liner crossing from Europe to the U.S. sinks in the middle of the Atlantic. Narrated by young newlywed Grace, one of thirty-nine survivors on an overcrowded lifeboat, the novel opens with her on trial for her life. We do not know why but learn in the prologue that one of Grace's lawyers has suggested she write her memoirs of the experience. Her story, which unfolds with the tension of a mystery, builds to the climactic event that resulted in Grace being on trial. She turns out to be an unreliable narrator, exposing herself as a calculating, self-serving person who, when the social order breaks down, looks out for her own welfare exclusively. The story pits the reader and Grace in a tense contest revolving around this question: How far will she (and did she) go to protect herself?

It's not an uplifting novel in any sense, as its portrait of human motivation is bleak and unflattering, suggesting we devolve to an animal state when social structures buckle and strain. This suggestion in no way accounts for the heroism and personal sacrifice for which humans are capable. Yet the novel is brilliantly executed and utterly gripping. Rogan's ability to evoke a visceral response through the quality and texture of her writing is nothing short of extraordinary.

The story explores an abundance of philosophical and historical questions: What is truth? What is the nature of the human condition? What happens when we strip away the trappings of civilization? Who will we become, and can we reconcile ourselves with this version of the self? Epically creepy, deeply dark, and profoundly disturbing, the novel provides an excellent model of the worst possible way to react when things fall apart.

The Giver by Lois Lowry

Like Bradbury's *Fahrenheit 451*, Lowry's novel for young readers is also often found on school curricula. On the cusp of turning twelve, Jonas, who lives with his mother, father, and younger sister, anticipates learning what his profession will be. In his society, childhood is considered over at the age of twelve. At an annual ceremony, he will be assigned a profession and then begin training for it. The community "elders" determine every aspect of citizens's lives, from how they speak, think, and dress to who they marry and how they spend every moment of their well-ordered lives. No detail has been left untended. Every action carries meaning and purpose, primarily to maintain order, safety, and control.

At the ceremony, Jonas learns he has been chosen as the Receiver of Memories. Though considered an honor, the "job," he is told, promises much pain and isolation and requires considerable bravery, which Jonas learns as he begins his training.

The current Receiver, who now calls himself the Giver, transfers memories to Jonas of how the world once was. "Before" included starvation, war, and pain, but it also contained beauty, art, and love, all of which were considered too dangerous and uncertain to be allowed to continue.

The book's overall message, that pain, wisdom, and beauty are bound up with each other in ways too essential to be unraveled, comes through in stark and elegant prose. It's a powerful message for children to carry into adulthood. It doesn't hurt to remind the grown-ups of it as well.

Hush by Jacqueline Woodson

Winner of a 2015 National Book Award for her memoir *Brown Girl Dreaming*, Woodson is a prolific author of children's and young adult fiction. In *Hush*, Toswiah Green is thirteen years old when her world changes forever. Her father, a Denver police officer who believes in his job, witnesses two white officers shoot and kill an unarmed black teen. Following his conscience, he testifies against the officers, and the fall-out for him and his family is swift, brutal, and irrevocable. The men who had been his brothers threaten the family, and after a bullet rips through the Greens's kitchen, they enter the Witness Protection program and are assigned new identities.

Cut off from all they have known, and adrift, Toswiah, her sister, and her parents suffer from the loss of self and community and struggle to reconcile with the consequences of doing the right thing. The novel highlights a difficult but crucial truth: To stand for justice is to choose the hard road, but it's the only road worth taking.

The Hunger Games by Suzanne Collins

The first novel in Suzanne Collins's young adult dystopian trilogy, *The Hunger Games* bears a resemblance to Shirley Jackson's short story "The Lottery." It has also been compared to the Japanese film *Battle Royale*, except this is a novel with a post-apocalyptic, teen gladiator twist. Katniss Everdeen is a hardscrabble, deprived fifteen-year-old living in a depraved world, who is chosen to take part in the book's titular games. The annual showdown leaves twenty-three children dead and is treated as what we can recognize as a perverse reality show, with interviews and stylists and directors who control the conditions of the "arena."

While the book's premise of children murdering each other is violent and disturbing, it raises important questions and issues, especially concerning how to cope in an imperfect world: How can we maintain our personal dignity and sense of moral authority when we're forced into situations that destroy it? To what extent are we able, practically speaking, to resist authority when it violates our sense of right and wrong? The book also reflects back at us our cultural obsession with reality television and the creepy way it transforms real people with real problems into playthings for our amusement. And it invites us to question to what degree we're complicit in creating a dystopic world when we allow complacency and judgment to replace agency and compassion.

Those We Love Most by Lee Woodruff

Maura and her husband Pete live a seemingly idyllic life with their three young children, but beneath the shiny veneer, fault lines threaten to burst apart in the wake of a shocking family tragedy. A parallel narrative follows Maura's parents, Roger and Margaret, who have been married for forty years but who harbor secrets that, once exposed, threaten the assumptions on which their marriage is based.

Sensitive and insightful, the novel prompts a host of thought-provoking questions, chief among them: How can families heal after catastrophic, life-altering events expose the flaws and limitations of each member? To what extent can we forgive ourselves our own mistakes and imperfections as well as those of our loved ones and move forward in a way that is hopeful?

World War Z: An Oral History of the Zombie War by Max Brooks

Composed of interviews conducted by an unnamed journalist with soldiers, scientists, and ordinary people from around the world who survived the zombie apocalypse, *World War Z: An*

Oral History of the Zombie War reads as a kind of thought experiment. At its center lies the question, How would a massive, *almost* impossible-to-defeat plague change how humans relate to each other and what they hold dear?

Brooks's imaginative vision is impressively epic in scope. The level of detail concerning how the "undead"—called "Zed Heads," "Zacks," and "Gs" by different groups—took over the world (including the oceans) and how difficult they are to defeat creates a convincing apocalyptic world. The stories the journalist collects as he travels across the globe highlight the resilience of the human spirit, as individuals, groups, and governments learn to collaborate in the face of near destruction. The stories illustrate the negative as well, especially how we tend to come together during a crisis but then fall apart again during the clean-up phase. Overall, it's an absorbing depiction of the human condition and our cycle of destruction and rebirth.

The Love Affairs of Nathaniel P.
by Adelle Waldman

Waldman's debut novel takes an at times chilling, at times hilarious, at times cringingly painful look into the mind of a young intellectual/writer through an anatomy of his five-month relationship with Hannah, who is *"almost universally regarded as nice and smart, or smart and nice."* Their relationship provides the perfect frame to explore a timeless question: Are men just jerks? Ha. I kid. The more mature articulation of the novel's underlying questions would be: To what extent can we control our likes and dislikes? How can we extricate ourselves with maturity, grace, and respect from relationships that are falling apart? And these questions apply, quite pointedly in Waldman's novel, to both genders.

While the story follows Nate and takes us deep into his experience, the narrator often assesses characters and situations at a slight remove from them, with the dispassionate air reminiscent of a therapist presenting a case study, and thus authorizes readers to do the same. Though the characters's behavior and choices can be almost excruciating at times, the book is insightfully observed and hilariously, skillfully rendered. In other words, Waldman provides reprieve from those dreadful moments with plenty of laugh-out-loud scenes.

CHAPTER 9

Books Set In Times of War – on the Battlefield and at Home

"A book must be the axe for the frozen sea within us."

– Franz Kafka

Of the many beloved books Judy Blume has written for children, it's strange that my favorite growing up was *Starring Sally J. Freedman as Herself*, which begins at a World War II Victory Day celebration. It's strange because, when I was rereading the novel until the covers fell off, I didn't know that my own relatives had lived through that same war not on U.S. soil but in Nazi-occupied Greece. As a child, I would often become exasperated at my grandmother's insistence that I finish every last morsel of food on my plate. I didn't understand why fiery arguments would erupt over a glass of unfinished orange juice or a half-eaten salad. I didn't understand that her aversion to wasting even one sip or one scrap was because she had survived famine and occupation. By the time I made the connection in adulthood, it was too late to ask her to tell me her stories.

Reading wartime novels and memoirs is one way I seek to pay tribute to her experience and to all those whose lives have been irrevocably altered or lost by war. Reading becomes, in these moments, a form of witnessing. This role has felt significant to me as a way to reach across the chasm that separates my experiences from those of my relatives who survived hardships I have never known. Though I won't ever claim to understand, viscerally, what they lived through, I can, at the very least, understand that I do not understand. These ten memoirs and novels, set on the war front and the home front, in wars on U.S. soil and beyond, all explore, in one way or another, the impact of war.

I Survived the Battle of Gettysburg, 1863 by Lauren Tarshis

As of this writing, Tarshis has published upwards of ten novels in her *I Survived* series for young readers. Elegantly written, with sensitivity, complexity, and a deep awareness of children's emotional lives, the books are meticulously researched and provide conversational starting points for parents and children.

In *I Survived the Battle of Gettysburg*, written to commemorate the one hundred fiftieth anniversary of the pivotal Civil War battle, eleven-year- old Thomas and his little sister Birdie are runaway slaves from a Virginia farm. We follow them as they fend off rebel soldiers, save the life of a Northern soldier, and travel with a Union military unit headed to Pennsylvania for the Battle of Gettysburg.

With nonstop action and vivid imagery, the novel is difficult to put down, even for grown-ups. But just as compelling is the emotional truth that good, bad, and indifferent exist in equal measure, and we can choose the path we take though it may be difficult, even heartbreaking. Like all the *I Survived* books, *The Battle of Gettysburg* is smart, nuanced, fast-paced, and deeply respectful of children's emotional lives, which also makes the novel valuable to adult readers.

A Farewell to Arms by Ernest Hemingway

Hemingway's iconic and gut-wrenching novel marries love story with war story, alternating between scenes of violence on the front and cozy domestic tableaux. Henry is an American serving in the Italian ambulance corps during World War I. After he is injured, he meets and falls in love with English nurse Catherine. In Hemingway's trademark stark prose, the novel moves back and forth between Henry's military experiences and his time with Catherine. Figurative language is nonexistent, yet we know everything (and more) that we need to know about what the characters are experiencing.

As a side note, F. Scott Fitzgerald collaborated with Hemingway on the ending, which the latter re-wrote thirty-nine times. If you can, get the version with the multiple endings. It's fascinating (and, for artists of any kind who have struggled to "get it right," inspiring) to see how the edits evolved into the final version.

I'll be Seeing You by Suzanne Hayes and Loretta Nyhan

Hayes and Nyhan wrote this epistolary novel before ever having met, just as their protagonists spend much of the novel as strangers in person but intimate in letters. The novel begins in

1943, when Glory and Rita, both wives of men serving overseas in World War II, meet through a service that pairs military wives as pen pals. The correspondence is meant to stave off the loneliness and anxiety of waiting, but the friendship that evolves between the two women goes much deeper as they become each other's confidants. Glory is a New England society lady and young mother struggling to manage two young children and the temptation of old love. Rita is an Iowa professor's wife whose steadfast devotion belies a more complicated past.

The novel's poignant first line, penned by Glory in her first letter to Rita—*"Dear 'Garden Witch,' I've stained my fingers blue trying to do this right"*—points to the difficulty and importance of breaking through our perfectionism and comfort zones in order to find connection.

A Soldier's Sketchbook: From the Front Lines of World War II by Joseph Farris

Long-time *New Yorker* cartoonist Farris was eighteen when he was drafted to serve in World War II and twenty-one when he returned home. His illustrated memoir captures the life of a common soldier serving in Europe through his wartime letters, photos, and sketches, which Farris had left unattended in a drawer for over sixty years.

Describing both battles and downtime in vivid detail, the carefully curated collection juxtaposes sunny letters home with news clippings revealing more dire conditions and features photos of ration kits and other daily realities of the era's soldiers. The memoir offers an affecting portrait of a soldier's wartime life.

Mare's War by Tanita S. Davis

This young adult novel begins with Mare and her two granddaughters, Octavia and Talitha, embarking on a summer road trip. The teens are accompanying their grandmother on a cross-country drive, from California to Alabama, for a family reunion. As they travel, Mare shares her wartime experiences with the girls. The narrative alternates between "now," with Mare, Octavia, and Talitha stopping at iconic locales across the country, and "then," when Mare served in the Women's Auxiliary Corps (WAC).

Though Davis did not base Mare on a single real-life WAC, she did draw on the real-life experiences of the 6888th Postal Battalion, in which eight hundred fifty-five African American women served. It was the first African American all-female battalion and the only one to be deployed overseas. In England, the 6888th worked three eight-hour shifts around the clock, sorting an overwhelming backlog of mail for the seven million United States Army, Navy, Marine Corps, civilian, and Red Cross personnel stationed in Europe.

Davis deftly weaves the 6888th's history into Mare's story, including her training and the bonds she develops with the other women, an Atlantic crossing fraught with danger (their carrier was tailed by German U-boats), and the struggles of daily life in wartime England. We're also confronted with the ugly realities of a segregated U.S. military, including separate housing, unequal treatment, and racial tension, in both the States and abroad. These invite characters, and readers, to reflect on the bitter irony of African American soldiers fighting for freedom in Europe though they are denied it at home.

Without giving too much away, *Mare's War* offers readers insight into African Americans's crucial contributions during WWII and how they would shape the years to come. It's also a compelling story of a woman reckoning with family bonds, her past, and how they have shaped her present.

Death in the Baltic by Cathryn Prince

Prince pulls a devastating disaster out of the shadow of history in this absorbing, heartbreaking, and sensitively written account of the 1945 sinking of the *Wilhelm Gustloff*. The one-time German cruise liner was carrying over ten thousand passengers, most of them civilians fleeing the Red Army's advance, when a Soviet submarine torpedoed it, resulting in over nine thousand deaths.

Why has this, the worst maritime disaster in history, been consigned to barely a footnote? Prince provides sociopolitical and historical context for both the disaster and the reasons it has been overlooked. Interwoven with the macro view of the disaster are first person accounts from survivors

who Prince interviewed, following them from the days leading up to the disaster through the bombing and its aftermath.
It's a thought-provoking and important book that deepens
our understanding of a defining period in world history.

The Things They Carried by Tim O'Brien

In addition to being a novelist and short story writer, O'Brien
is a Vietnam veteran. *The Things They Carried* is a collection
of interrelated war stories based on his experiences in Vietnam.
Though seemingly autobiographical, with a narrator who
shares the same name as the author, the book refuses easy cat-
egorization and is credited with introducing a new genre: the
fiction/memoir hybrid. This genre boundary crossing is purposeful. It reflects the author's complicated relationship with
truth: *"I want you to feel what I felt,"* he writes. *"I want you to
know why story-truth is truer sometimes than happening-truth."*

The stories follow a platoon of Vietnam War soldiers, delving deep into their hearts and minds in prose whose lyricism
juxtaposes the harsh reality it portrays.

The Cellist of Sarajevo by Stephen Galloway

Galloway's novel follows the fates of four people in the city
of Sarajevo during the siege that lasted almost four years. At
the center of the story is the cellist, who sees from his window
twenty-two friends and neighbors killed in a mortar attack as

SALLY ALLEN

they wait on a bread line. He resolves to play at the site of the shelling for twenty-two days. Unbeknownst to him, a sniper is hired to ensure his safety, which implies the existence of others whose goal is to ensure that his gesture of hope ends prematurely. Elsewhere in the city, a man leaves his wife and children to undertake a treacherous journey for water, and a shell-shocked man searching for bread runs into an old friend who reminds him of the city (and self) he feared he has lost forever.

It's good that I'm writing, rather than speaking, about this lyrical, haunting, but ultimately uplifting novel. Speaking would be difficult given the lump that takes up residence in my throat whenever I think about this book. It explores the effect of war on our sense of community and self as well as art's ability to heal and restore. It spotlights the atrocities particular to Sarajevo and invites questions about why the siege continued for so long. But it also shows how the machine of war, any war, becomes divorced from the cost to the human spirit.

The Song of Achilles by Madeline Miller

The wartime setting in this book reaches all the way back to ancient times: the Trojan War. The novel reframes *The Iliad* as a love story told from the perspective of Patrocles, Achilles's companion in the epic poem. The two first meet after a young Patrocles is sent into exile for accidentally killing another child and finds a home in the court of Achilles's father. *The Song of Achilles* follows their growing bond as children, eventual love as adolescents and adults, and interdependence at Troy, building towards Achilles's fateful decision to allow Patrocles to fight wearing his lover's armor.

Miller's writing evokes the musicality of the original epic poem. Besides that, she manages to make the ancient world feel both far away and accessible at the same time by infusing alien customs with familiar emotions. Her novel also inspired me to reread parts of *The Iliad*, a book I hadn't read since high school.

Ransom by David Malouf

This lyrical novel is also set during the Trojan War. It offers a fresh take on the story of Achilles and King Priam from books sixteen to twenty-four of *The Iliad*, in which Priam of Troy brings the Greek warrior a ransom (hence the title) to recover the body of his son Hector.

At the novel's outset, Achilles has killed Hector in battle to avenge the death of Patrocles at the hands of Hector. But so deep is Achilles's grief and rage at the loss of his partner that he defiles Hector's body, tying it to the back of his chariot and dragging it through the dirt (symbolism alert). Yet each day he wakes up to find, frustratingly enough, that the gods have restored Hector's corpse to its pre-defiled condition, presumably in protest of Achilles's out-of-bounds actions.

Meanwhile, behind the walls of Troy, Priam hatches an unorthodox plan to recover his son's corpse so that it can be properly buried. Rather than demanding the body as a king, Priam intends to humble himself before the great warrior by dressing in plain garments and riding into the Greek camp on a simple cart driven by a mule. Of course, there will also be treasures, which Priam will offer in exchange for Hector's body.

Priam's wife and family are alarmed at his plan, in particular this disturbing insinuation: *"[T]here may be another way of naming what we call fortune and attribute to the will, or the whim, of the gods. Which offers a kind of opening. The opportunity to act for ourselves. To try something different that might force events into a different course."* Priam believes that his eccentric plan provides an opportunity for immortality through actions that will be remembered and talked about long after he is gone. He moves forward with his intention, selecting as a companion on his journey a common middle-aged cart driver, Somax, chosen randomly from the market. Much of the novel follows the two as they attempt to reach the Greek camp safely, without negative interference from either Greek or god, and the bond they develop.

CHAPTER 10

Novels That Explore Russian Life Before and After the Soviet Revolution

"There is no subject so old that something new cannot be said about it."

– Fyodor Dostoyevsky

Growing up, I knew of the Soviet Union as the *other* world power, the one said to have bread lines, comrades, and the world's best pairs figure skaters. It wasn't until a world history class in high school that I learned about pre-Soviet history and the Bolshevik Revolution. I was especially haunted by a photo in my textbook of the Romanov daughters, ghostly in their gauzy white dresses and poofy hair, gazing mournfully at the camera as if they intuited their fate. This was also when I discovered that pre-Soviet Russians and I shared a religion in common: Eastern Orthodox Christianity. Perhaps this is why I have felt at home in Russian literature. The first time I met an Eastern Orthodox literary character was when I read, in graduate school, *Crime and Punishment* by Fyodor Dostoyevsky. I had never seen my religious customs and rites depicted on the page before and felt the thrill of recognition and connection.

Russian literature also resonates with me on a soul level because of the way classic Russian authors I have read and loved frame suffering as not only inescapable but also potentially redeeming. Rather than portraying it as an unfortunate aspect of life that we either have to just endure or try to resist, my favorite Russian classics show how suffering is an indispensible part of how we might come into our best selves. Exploring aspects of Russian life before, during, and after the Bolshevik Revolution, the following ten books inspire readers to consider suffering as an essential counterpoint to joy and beauty.

Eugene Onegin by Alexander Pushkin

I put off reading *Eugene Onegin*, Pushkin's novel in verse, for years owing to anxiety about poetry, but when I finally sat down with James E. Falen's translation, it enchanted and entranced me. With the mood of a fable, it tells the story of the eponymous Onegin, a young man who has grown bored with society life and given up on passion and emotion, and his doomed friendship with Lensky, an innocent poet who has not yet shed his youthful ideals. He falls in love with Olga, a flighty young girl whose sister Tatyana falls in love with Onegin. A fictionalized Pushkin narrates their stories. Interspersed with his reflections on the nature of love, ennui, the "Russian soul," and the individual in society are the events in which these play out.

The musicality of Pushkin's iambic tetrameter pushes against the melancholy and tragedy of the story, echoing the contradictory nature of the human animal as brought to life by the author. The novel carried me along in its currents, in the end provoking, appropriately enough, the contradictory emotions of pleasure in the writing and sadness at what it reveals about our natures.

The Master and Margarita by Mikhail Bulgakov

Born in Kiev in 1891, Bulgakov worked on his satiric masterpiece during uncertain and troubling times in the new Soviet state: He began it in 1928 and worked on it until his death in 1940, having taken time off to burn the manuscript in despair over the prospects for writers in the Soviet Union. Both laugh-out-loud funny and philosophical, the novel explores the inter-relation of good and evil, borrowing themes from Faust and boasting characters named with Dickensian intention.

The book alternates between two settings—contemporary Moscow (i.e. the 1930s) and Jerusalem in the time of Pontius Pilate. When the novel opens, the devil arrives in Moscow in the guise of a foreign professor named Woland, whose retinue includes Behemoth (a large black cat who can walk on two legs and speak), Azazello (a hitman who sports fangs and has a wandering eye), Abadonna (a ghostly pale figure), and Hella (a flame-haired vampire). Most of the novel follows them as they wreak havoc on the city and its residents, exposing the new elite's vanity and greed, engaging in philosophical debates, and playing all manner of tricks.

Among the objects of their pranks are Berlioz, the head of the literary elite and their cumbersome bureaucracy, and Ivan Ponyrev, a poet who lands in an insane asylum. There, he meets the Master, a disillusioned and embittered author who burned his manuscript (a novel about the meeting between Pontius Pilate and Yeshua Ha-Notsri). Also figuring into the story is Margarita, the master's steadfast lover who plays a re-demptive role.

Choosing the best English translation among the many that exist is a topic of much debate among readers. I enjoyed both the Penguin Classic translated by Richard Pevear and Larissa Volokhonsky and the 1967 translation by Mirra

Ginsburg, though I preferred Ginsburg's slightly because it conveyed more humor. A word of caution: Ginsburg's translation is of the censored Soviet version of the novel. And now for a fun fact about *The Master and Margarita*: It inspired the Rolling Stones song "Sympathy with the Devil."

And Quiet Flows the Don by Mikhail Sholokhov

This novel, translated into English by Stephen Garry, follows the fates and fortunes of the Don Cossacks during the early years of the twentieth century, from the period before World War I through the Russian Revolution and Russian civil war. Written between 1928 and 1940, the novel is considered a seminal work of socialist realism and was awarded the Nobel Prize in Literature in 1965. I should also note that some scholars have argued that the novel is the work of multiple authors.

The story revolves around a Cossack family, particularly one Grigory Panteleevich Melekhov, who undergoes a significant transformation, and includes scenes of horrific brutality, violence against women, and anti-Semitism. Rendered with much unadorned description, the narrative style is somewhat reminiscent of Hemingway. Simplicity and directness are hallmarks of both, but where simplicity for Hemingway seems to strive to bring us closer to the emotional truth of a moment, simplicity for Sholokhov seems to strive for rationality and to conquer sentimentality.

Scenes of bald description can go on for pages, casting moments of narrative judgment into relief. For example, as Grigory is fulfilling his military requirement just before the outbreak of World War I, his thoughts are revealed with an intimacy out of step with the blunt accounting of most of the narrative: *"As Grigory glanced at the polished, well-groomed officers in their handsome grey greatcoats and closely-fitting uniforms, he felt that there was an impassable wall between them and himself. Their very different, comfortable, well-ordered existence, so unlike that of the Cossacks, flowed on peacefully, untroubled by mud, lice, or fear of the sergeant-major's fists."*

Though I wouldn't call it exactly enjoyable to read, *And Quiet Flows the Don* is an important novel about a pivotal group of historical players during a crucial moment in history. I would especially recommend it for those interested in Russian and Soviet history and literature.

Mastering the Art of Soviet Cooking: A Memoir of Food and Longing by Anya Von Bremzen

In 1974, Von Bremzen emigrated from the Soviet Union to the U.S. with her mother. Her memoir tells the story of the rise and fall of America's one-time nemesis and the character of its people through an exploration of its food. Interlaced with this investigation are her family's stories and what it looked like and meant to grow up and live during various stages of the U.S.S.R.'s evolution.

She moves seamlessly among Soviet history, food, and personal anecdotes, convincingly establishing food as a revelatory cultural artifact and receptacle for beliefs and values. And while seventy years seems like a lot of ground to cover in a three hundred thirty-three page book, Von Bremzen succinctly captures key historical moments through judicious curating, inevitably moving beyond food but also using it to ground the overall narrative. Family anecdotes, food-related and otherwise, are lavishly developed, and the memoir as a whole oozes tragicomic irony redolent of a Russian novel.

About that last bit: Studying history—of the Soviet Union and otherwise—promises an almost endless parade of atrocities. How do we confront them? Options include mining them for morbid humor or losing your ever-loving mind. Von Bremzen, in the great Russian literary tradition, is a master of the former. And on top of it all, her book radiates lovingness, an ability survivors have for finding beauty and meaning in the bleakest of places.

Doctor Zhivago by Boris Pasternak

Doctor Zhivago follows Yuri Zhivago from his childhood in Tsarist Russia to his experiences during and after the Bolshevik Revolution of 1917, along with his wife Tonya, his lover Larissa, and, as is typical of the great Russian epics, an overwhelmingly massive cast of characters (it helps to keep a list).

Before reading Pevear and Volokhonsky's translation, I could not comprehend, in a visceral way, the appeal of Communism and why the Revolution succeeded. I could name the reasons from history books, but I could not empathize, which is to say, I could not put myself in the mind and heart of someone experiencing that moment in history.

Through its in-depth portrayal of so many characters's inner lives, Pasternak's novel gave me that ability to *feel*, finally, what made the Revolution so compelling, the euphoria of its ideals, and then also the disillusionment that followed their implementation. Whatever readers and scholars argue about the novel's literary merits (and they have debated them from the beginning), it enabled me to experience something previously elusive, and for that reason, it is quite dear to me.

The Zhivago Affair: The Kremlin, the CIA, and the Battle Over a Forbidden Book by Peter Finn and Petra Couvée

I eagerly anticipated the release of *The Zhivago Affair*. It tells the story of the novel *Dr. Zhivago* through the story of its author, Boris Pasternak, as well as the Italian publisher who carried the novel out of the U.S.S.R. and the Soviet officials and CIA operatives who believed in the book's power as an ideological tool.

It begins with Pasternak, who believed his novel would never be accepted for publication in the Soviet Union. Visited by the agent of a Communist Italian publisher hoping to receive the foreign rights to the book, Pasternak, who saw fellow writers disappear during the purges of the 1930s, handed him the manuscript, saying, *"'You are hereby invited to my execution.'"*

The drama that unfolds around the book and its publication has, at times, the mood of a suspense thriller. What is perhaps most striking to me is how one novel could inspire such anxiety, passion, fear, and determination. That it did, speaks to the power literature has to transform us—precisely what I experienced first-hand reading *Doctor Zhivago*. I also couldn't help thinking, as I read *The Zhivago Affair*, about the darker implications of that power.

Winter Garden by Kristin Hannah

In Hannah's novel, sisters Meredith and Nina live opposite lives. Meredith married young, raised two daughters, and takes care of her parents and the family business, while Nina has chosen a rootless life, traveling the world (and war zones) as a photojournalist. One thing they do share is the pain of having grown up feeling unloved by their emotionally distant mother, Anya, a Russian émigré brought to the U.S. after World War II by her serviceman husband.

On his deathbed, Meredith and Nina's father asks them to find out their mother's story, and this sends the three women on a journey both emotional and literal. We travel back to

Leningrad during the siege and to contemporary Alaska to uncover both what happened to Anya during the war, and the events's long-lasting repercussions on her. What all three women discover forces them to reinterpret the past and re-shape the present in this affecting novel that exposes the brutal conditions in Leningrad during World War II and that has more than one shocking reveal.

The Man From St. Petersburg by Ken Follett

It's 1914 in London, and Europe is on the brink of a war that will topple empires and usher in sweeping social change across the globe. Against this backdrop, Winston Churchill and Lord Walden arrange a hush-hush meeting with Russian Prince Aleks Orlov to secure an alliance between the two world powers. But an anarchist on the run from St. Petersburg heads for London with other plans for his homeland, and he has a hidden connection to Walden's Russian-born wife, Lydia. Pulled into this conflict is her daughter, Charlotte, who, at eighteen, is preparing for her entry into Society, but experiencing intellectual and moral awakenings that test her loyalties.

The Man from St. Petersburg is chock full of well-paced tension and nail-biting chase scenes, but the story's heart-beat lies in the pressure that secrets bring to bear on human relationships. Follett provides plenty of plot points and scenes that demonstrate secrecy's devastating effects, from outright lying to lying by omission. He also, as the novel progresses, invites readers to question our values and character loyalties. Just when he has us thinking one way, he pulls us in the other direction. The novel's action and tension do get the heart racing. But its ideas and debates, including those related to the Bolshevik Revolution, leave the most long-lasting effects and kept my mind spinning long after I'd read the last page.

City of Thieves by David Benioff

This novel by the acclaimed screenwriter features a meta narrative frame: A first-person narrator named David, who lives in Los Angeles and is a screenwriter, reminisces about his grandfather, a Russian immigrant who will share only the bare bones of his Soviet wartime experiences. When David asks for more details, his grandfather tells him, "'*You're a writer. Make it up.*'"

With that, we travel back to June 1941 and the siege of Leningrad, where Lev Beniov, in the wrong place at the wrong time, is arrested for looting and thrown into the same cell as Kolya, a deserter. The two are given one chance to save their lives: Procure a dozen eggs for a powerful Soviet colonel, who needs them to have a cake baked for his daughter's wedding. Their journey takes Lev and Kolya into the shadowy corners of lawless Leningrad and behind German lines, but it's not a dark novel. It's packed with thrills, near misses, tragedy, black comedy, and a sense of hope in the individual spirit.

The Possessed: Adventures with Russian Books and the People Who Read Them by Elif Batuman

Smart, funny, and melancholy, Batuman's memoir melds literary journalism and analysis with deeply revealing personal stories. She writes about classic Russian authors (Tolstoy, Pushkin, Dostoyevsky) in a way that's familiar to me from my own days as a graduate student. But you don't have to be an academic to appreciate her storytelling, which quietly echoes the kind of wry observations and pathos-filled characters you might find in some of the Russian novels she discusses. Her exquisitely crafted scenes include a summer spent studying in Uzbekistan, an Isaac Babel conference, and her pilgrimage to St. Petersburg to visit a replica of the 1740 House of Ice, originally created at the behest of Empress Anna, niece of Peter the Great.

In recounting her adventures, Batuman reveals her awareness of the absurd, the beautiful, and their cohabitation. And she has one of the best last lines I have ever read in a book of this kind, which I promise won't spoil it for you: *"If I could start over today, I would choose literature again. If the answers exist in the world or in the universe, I still think that's where we're going to find them."*

CHAPTER 11

Books That Explore University Life

*"All that mankind has done, thought,
gained, or been; it is lying as in magic
preservation in the pages of books."*

– Thomas Carlyle

When I imagined life as a professor, I imagined leisurely hours spent pouring over books, soul-nurturing conversations with bright-eyed students and brilliant colleagues, sunlight streaming through stained glass windows set in buildings draped in ivy. I imagined an ivory tower tucked away from the unsavory aspects of contemporary life, like commercialism and the need for self-promotion. No one would ever be exploited or be at the mercy of someone's personal whims or require currency. Apparently, I cultivated the hope that being at a university transforms humans into mythical beings.

You may be surprised to hear that my fantasy has not been fully realized. It turns out that the university, like any other institution organized, administered, and populated by humans, has its flaws. It also has its joys, notably, those soul-nurturing conversations mentioned above, of which I've enjoyed many. Should you be interested in delving into some of these flaws and joys, they are beautifully illuminated, to varying degrees, in these ten books.

The Marriage Plot by Jeffrey Eugenides

The Marriage Plot offers an intense character study revolving around three friends who meet at Brown University in 1982. Leonard is the deeply troubled bad boy with whom Madeleine is in love, while spiritual seeker Mitchell holds a candle for Madeleine. An absorbing and melancholy reflection on growing up and older, the novel explores what remains after stark realities chip away at the shiny veneer of youthful enthusiasm and we're left to live with our choices. I wouldn't call it cynical ... exactly.

The title's clever literary reference—to the prominence of courtship and marriage storylines in eighteenth- and nineteenth-century novels—is the first clue that Eugenides knows his way around literary history and theory. English majors may particularly appreciate the primer, revealed through Madeleine's experience as a literature student. Reading the novel helped me understand the evolution of English studies and how it came to be what it was by the time I hit graduate school. I found myself identifying with Madeleine in this moment early in the book: *"Madeleine had a feeling that most semiotic theorists had been unpopular as children, often bullied or overlooked, and so had directed their lingering rage onto literature. They wanted to demote the author. [...] They wanted the reader to be the main thing. Because they were the readers."*

Pnin by Vladimir Nabokov

A character-driven novel if ever there was one, *Pnin* follows the misadventures of Timofey Pavlovich Pnin, a Russian émigré teaching Russian literature at fictional Waindell College in the 1950s. For much of this novel, in which the narrator is as significant as the character whose story he's telling, not much happens by way of plot. But who cares? I was swept away by the beauty of the language and the way it makes me see the world in a way I never would have if left to my own devices. For example: *"With the help of the janitor he screwed onto the side of the desk a pencil sharpener— that highly satisfying, highly philosophical implement that goes Ticonderoga-ticon-deroga, feeding on the yellow finish and sweet wood, and ends up in a kind of soundlessly spinning ethereal void as we all must."*

About two-thirds of the way in, the novel takes a turn, becoming rife with page-turning campus politics and intrigue. Though Nabokov isn't one for shiny, happy endings, his brilliant turns of phrase, laser-sharp observations, and gift for telling details make the heart soar, even while it's breaking for the characters.

The Physick Book of Deliverance Dane by Katherine Howe

I found this novel on the shelves at Barnes & Nobles during an idle stroll through the fiction section. The cover claimed the book was "spooky," which is at the top of my list of favorite words (though I tend steer clear of reads that fall into the horror genre). The novel tells the story of Connie Goodwin, a Ph.D. candidate in history searching for a unique primary source around which to conduct her dissertation research. She finds that source when she returns to her grandmother's home, abandoned for twenty years after her death: a family artifact (the "physick" book referenced in the title) with an unexpected connection to the Salem Witch Trials.

Howe, who is descended from three women tried for witchcraft during the Salem Witch Trials (one of whom was executed), intersects Connie's story with selective narratives from the past. We know more than Connie does, but not enough to uncover the secret of the document around which her dissertation revolves. Like Connie, we're trying to piece together the data to arrive at a conclusion. It's an enthralling, suspenseful read—especially for history buffs—with a side helping of magical realism and romance.

Wonder Boys by Michael Chabon

Chabon is a master of "dude lit," characterized by muscular prose and plot intensity, with a pinch of sardonic wit and a dose of male angst. *Wonder Boys* has these in spades. An author and professor at a Pittsburgh college, Grady Tripp enjoyed wonder boy status with an award-winning novel, but seven years later, he's struggling with an unwieldy two-thousand-plus-page follow-up that won't behave. His wife has left him, his lover (the college's chancellor) is pregnant, and one of his talented young students goes off the rails in a big way. And all this on the eve of WordFest, an authors and publishers week-end event the college is sponsoring.

Lo, the many hijinks that ensue! Despite some bad (and bizarre) behavior, the characters endeared themselves to me, helped along by the many laughs I enjoyed at their expense. Overall, the novel offers a hugely entertaining romp through the wacky world of academe.

Dear Committee Members by Julie Schumacher

This epistolary novel tells the story of literature in the university through sixty-plus letters of recommendation written by beleaguered English and Creative Writing professor and floundering novelist Jason Fitger over the course of one academic year. As the year (and the novel) begins, the graduate English program has been defunded, departed full-time English faculty have been replaced with adjuncts, and the building in which the department is housed is under construction to benefit the well-funded Economics faculty.

Fitger's letters are addressed to various and sundry, from university administrators, his literary agent, and a writing residency director, to personnel in food services, child care, and a paintball company, among others. Written on behalf of students and colleagues, the letters raise legitimate questions about the place of literature and the functioning of academic life. At times bizarre and confessional, Fitger's missives reveal him to be an egoist and a windbag prone to self-destructive personal diversions. But he is also a man with an abiding faith in art and beauty and an admirably low tolerance for posturing and politicking. Those of us who believe in literature's power to sustain and inspire might find in *Dear Committee Members* a kind of call to arms. At the very least, we might hear in Fitger's endearments and pronouncements a faith worth advocating for: *"I am [...] not afraid or ashamed to be a dinosaur, a person who reads and teaches novels (not 'texts'), and who instills whenever possible during class sessions a fast-fading (and, to the students, possibly retrograde or endearing) humanistic agenda, emphasizing literary inquiry into the human experience and the human condition."*

The Sixteenth of June by Maya Lang

Like James Joyce's *Ulysses*, which inspired Lang's novel, *The Sixteenth of June* takes place over the course of a single day, June sixteenth. Events unfold from the start of the day and alternate points of view among brothers Stephen and Leopold (named by their parents for Joyce's protagonists) and Nora, best friend of the former and fiancée of the latter. Their narratives carry us from their morning rituals as they prepare for the funeral of the men's grandmother, through the funeral, and to the party held by Stephen and Leopold's striver parents for Bloomsday, an annual celebration of James Joyce.

Oldest son Stephen is a graduate student struggling to write his dissertation and questioning his sense of purpose as an academic. His younger brother Leopold is an IT consultant who enjoys beer and sports and longs both for acceptance from his parents and a more "normal" life. Nora, a talented opera singer, had a promising career on the horizon but abandoned this path following her mother's death and is beset by crippling anxiety. As the day's events unfold, revelations and realizations lead each character to grapple with his or her interpretations both of the present and the past.

The Sixteenth of June is my favorite kind of novel—one that acknowledges the chaos and imperfection of the human condition and communication, while still locating the possibility for hope within the mess. It's a novel about the intersection of stories, about the search for personal meaning and fulfillment in the face of our interconnectedness, about the difficulty of coming to terms with who you are in relation to those around you.

A Jane Austen Education: How Six Novels Taught Me About Love, Friendship, and the Things That Really Matter by William Deresiewicz

Deresiewicz's memoir was part of my 2013 Year of Jane Austen, my personal celebration of the two hundredth anniversary of *Pride and Prejudice*. It consisted of reading Jane Austen, Jane Austen fan fiction, and Jane Austen memoirs, including *A Jane Austen Education*.

In this book, Deresiewicz tells his personal story through the lens of his reading Austen's novels. Each novel corresponds to a stage of his adulthood, including his time as a graduate student and graduate teaching assistant. The lessons Austen's heroines learn are often mirrored in those Deresiewicz himself absorbs—in his judgments of others, his willingness to love, and his need to embrace further learning. Copious and engaging literary analysis and history reveal the connection between Deresiewicz and Austen's characters, and his reading of the novels is insightful and interesting. Also, it's inspiring to see a twenty-first-century dude relating to and learning from the experiences of early nineteenth-century female heroines. If this doesn't illustrate the power of literature to connect us, I don't know what will.

My Life in Middlemarch by Rebecca Mead

Mead's memoir is a book to savor. The longtime *New Yorker* writer crafts beautiful prose and an elegant story about growing into adulthood with George Eliot's *Middlemarch* as her beloved, defining, frequently reread novel.

Mead's story begins during her adolescence, when she first discovered George Eliot's classic novel while being tutored for her university entrance exams. At that point in her life, itching to move forward, eager to leave her provincial seaside town, Mead identified with the novel's heroine, Dorothea Brooke, who also longs for more. After Mead goes off to university, then embarks on a career that sends her to glamorous cities around the world, the novel grows with her, as she discovers deeper wisdoms with each rereading.

In addition to personal anecdotes and reflections, the memoir provides a deep reading of Eliot the woman and author, owing to Mead's considerable historical research and analysis of the novel itself. Her memoir might also inspire readers to read, or reread, *Middlemarch*, which is a pleasure to see anew through Mead's eyes.

Elizabeth the First Wife by Lian Dolan

Featuring sharp dialogue and dynamic prose, and populated by endearingly human characters, *Elizabeth the First Wife* follows community college Shakespeare professor Elizabeth Lancaster. Elizabeth is the youngest daughter in a family of overachievers: Her father is a Nobel Prize winner, one sister is a cancer researcher, and the other is the wife of a California congressman considering a run for governor. Even her ex-husband, action movie superstar FX Fahey, outshines her. But though her life has stalled in her mid-thirties, Elizabeth is happy ... mostly. She loves where and who she teaches and is surrounded by loving friends and family, even if her mother does continually browbeat her about pursuing more in her career and personal life. In part to get her mother off her back, Elizabeth resolves to flesh out an idea for a book about modern relationships using Shakespeare couples as models. Between each chapter in Dolan's novel is a fictional page from Elizabeth's book-within-a-book, and they are laugh-out-loud funny, as is most of the novel itself.

Elizabeth's book project dovetails into another opportunity: FX asks her to join him at a Shakespeare festival, where he will be performing in an avant-garde production of *A Midsummer Night's Dream*. She agrees, and her life takes a turn for the exciting. The briskly plotted novel takes off from there with hilarious twists and turns, including a big one that completely surprised me. And I'm pretty tough to sneak up on. The twist made perfect sense, and that I didn't see it coming is a tribute to how engaging Dolan's world is. I didn't stop to think about what would come next; I just threw myself into the narrative. And the Bard is not just a handy plot device. From the first page to the last, Dolan cleverly infuses Shakespeare plots and characters in contemporary form. But perhaps the best part of all is seeing a down-to-earth academic fulfilled by and happy with her teaching.

Wittgenstein Jr by Lars Iyer

Iyer's lyrical novel unfolds like a prose poem, in fragments and scenes, compressed images and emotional tones. The story concerns a group of Cambridge students on the cusp of entering the real world, and their philosophy lecturer (whom they dub "Wittgenstein"), who is on the cusp of madness.

The first-person narrator is known as "Peters." Hailing from the north of England, he seems to be something of an enigma to his classmates, who represent a cross-section of English society. Peters's narrative alternates between classroom scenes—in which a frustrated Wittgenstein rails against Logic, the Cambridge dons, philosophy, and his students, who are both confused and intrigued by their increasingly unhinged lecturer—and scenes of college debauchery. The students drink and drug in excess as they playact scenes from philosophical texts (Socrates's death, for example) and contemplate their uncertain futures.

Mirroring the characters's precarious existential states is the story's shifting focus. It is at turns a novel about England, university life, youth, madness, philosophy, and love, which, when summed up, becomes a compelling coming-of-age novel.

CHAPTER 12

Novels That Thrill, Chill, and Keep You Guessing

"To learn to read is to light a fire; every syllable that is spelled out is a spark."

– Victor Hugo

When I was in middle school, I enjoyed reading Agatha Christie novels. Trying to piece together the clues to solve the murder was absorbing, as if I myself were in a battle of wits and nerve with the unknown assailant. The exercise required my full concentration and attention, thus providing a therapeutic escape from the predictable dramas associated with middle school life. In those instances when my detective work proved sound, and I was able to predict who the murderer was, I felt the pleasure of accomplishment in having successfully solved the crime. And when I didn't get it right, I could still enjoy the closure of seeing a mystery explained. This kind of closure can be elusive in real life, which is precisely why it can be so satisfying in a book.

As an adult, I gravitated away from thrillers and mysteries and more toward literary fiction, until I discovered John le Carré, whose books encompass qualities of both. Reading literary fiction, I tend to let the story wash over me and gradually come together. But reading le Carré took me back to the pleasure of that other way of reading, of noting pointed details, bookmarking pages, trying to anticipate the next twist. We might need to work actively at the puzzle when we read books like this, keeping our wits about us so no clue escapes, but we can also feel enlivened by the vicarious danger and discovery. From action-packed thrillers to psychological mysteries, the following ten books invite us to let go of certainty and lose ourselves in the chase.

The Spy Who Came in From the Cold
by John le Carré

Le Carré rocks this genre with smart, thrilling action, fully developed characters, moral dilemmas, gorgeous, elegant writing, and so much tension you could pass out for forgetting to breathe. The best example of his virtuosity may well be *The Spy Who Came in From the Cold*, first published in 1963. The novel begins and ends in East Germany during a particularly tense period of the Cold War. A double agent is shot dead attempting to defect, and in West Berlin, the British Secret Intelligence Service stews as it tallies its losses. Station Head Alec Leamas is recalled to London and offered an opportunity to redeem himself by going up against the deadly leader of the East German Secret Service, Hans-Dieter Mundt.

Critics have called *The Spy Who Came in From the Cold* the best spy novel of all time, and I am inclined to agree. It fulfills all the spy thriller criteria with tremendous skill and intelligence. But it's also a deeply felt and empathetic portrait of Leamas, a man trapped in the lies he has constructed, unable to break free of his past, struggling against a sense of failure and isolation. It casts a shrewd eye on the moral and ethical debates of the profession and the period, pushing readers into shadowy corners where we're forced to confront how far we—and our governments—are willing to go to protect our interests.

The End of Everything by Megan Abbott

This novel centers on the narrator, Lizzie, who is thirteen years old when the story begins, and her best friend since early childhood, Evie Verver. Lizzie believes she and Evie share everything, from clothes and activities to sleepovers and secrets. But then Evie vanishes, and Lizzie is forced to reconcile her conscious beliefs about their relationship with her subconscious recognition that things were not quite what they seemed, nor what she wanted them to be.

Though its protagonists are young adults, *The End of Everything* isn't labeled young adult fiction, and it's interesting to read about the adolescent experience as it's portrayed for an adult audience rather than for a peer audience. One striking difference is that we're invited, along with the grown-up Lizzie narrating the story, to reckon with choices after their consequences have already been felt rather than in the moments when they're playing out. Abbott is an accomplished mystery writer, and *The End of Everything* is partly a mystery, as Lizzie investigates what may have happened to Evie and why, collecting physical and emotional clues. But it's also about what happens when tragedy exposes the fissures in our governing illusions about the world.

The Cutting Season by Attica Locke

This engaging thriller has earned rave reviews from readers and critics for combining a page-turning murder mystery with an incisive look at race, politics, and power. The novel is set on a Louisiana plantation called Belle Vie. In the present day, Caren Grey, the descendent of slaves who worked its fields, manages the operations of the property as a tourist attraction. Preserved as it stood in the antebellum South, Belle Vie is used for weddings and parties. At the story's outset, the body of a murdered migrant worker is found on the plantation's grounds, inviting parallels to the one hundred thirty-seven year-old unsolved murder of one of Caren's ancestors. Drawn into the investigation, Caren is forced to grapple with her distant and recent pasts and their implications on her daughter's future.

Well-plotted and complex (pay attention to everything!), the novel asks difficult but important questions that defy easy answers—about the conditions migrant workers endure, about what makes a family, and about what power we have in the face of things we cannot change.

We Were Liars by E. Lockhart

Narrated by seventeen-year-old Cady Sinclair, this young adult novel is her journey to uncover the details behind the accident that left her with crippling headaches and significant memory loss. At the novel's outset, Cady remembers nothing about her fifteenth summer, other than that she was found half-dressed and half-submerged in the ocean. How she got there is revealed in pieces, through a fragmented narrative that at times evokes the spare qualities of a modernist poem.

Lockhart clocks the reader with a shocking reveal at the end of this carefully constructed, fable-like story that delves into the relationship between Cady, her two cousins, and a family friend. The foursome grew up spending their summers on the private island of Cady's Boston Brahmin grandparents. Careful readers may foresee the ending—the clues are all there—but even readers for whom the ending has been spoiled have much to contemplate.

Mission to Paris by Alan Furst

Set in Paris in 1938 with Europe on the brink of war, the novel tells the story of Austrian-born Hollywood film star Fredric Stahl, who travels to the city to film a movie set during World War I. In Paris, the Nazis have already begun to wage political warfare designed to weaken French morale, and they seek to recruit Stahl for their efforts. But the actor has other ideas, and he takes on an espionage mission at the American embassy's behest. Meanwhile, he negotiates invitations from German sympathizers in Paris, some of whom may not be what they seem. And he might be falling in love with one of the women in his orbit.

The novel is brilliantly paced as Stahl attempts to step around the landmines that the Germans, who are determined to use him, place in his path. As the dangers increase, so does the tempo. Be prepared to be glued to this book until the last word.

The Paris Deadline by Max Byrd

Can a thriller be warm-hearted? *The Paris Deadline*, set between the two World Wars, certainly is. An eighteenth-century automaton, thought to be a reproduction of Vaucanson's Duck, lands in the hands of Toby Keats, World War I veteran and Paris reporter for a Chicago newspaper. The duck is sought after by a number of people, including American Ph.D. Elsie Short and a band of European baddies who want to sell it to the Germans as they prepare for war. Keats uses his journalistic skills to uncover why the duck is so desired, whether it's a fake, and what other secrets it's connected to, running into quite a few surprises along the way.

Providing heart-stopping action and a fascinating peek into news delivery during the early twentieth century, the novel also features beautifully developed, loveable characters from whom I was sad to be parted after reading the final page.

You Are One of Them by Elliot Holt

Fearing nuclear war in 1982, two ten-year-old girls, Sarah Zuckerman and Jenny Jones, write letters to Soviet politician Yuri Andropov. While Sarah never receives a response, Jenny's letter is answered and catapults her to international attention until her death in a mysterious plane crash in 1985. But did she really die? A decade later, Sarah receives a letter from Russia that casts doubt on the official record, and she travels to Moscow to find out the truth.

Holt's novel, inspired by a true story, has the cadence of a thriller but the mood of a meditation—on friendship, truth, loss, and the illusions we carry about ourselves and those who we believe are closest to us.

Trapeze by Simon Mawer

Volumes of historical nonfiction have been written chronicling the experiences of women spies during World War II. I love how looking at their stories together provides a panoramic view, like a camera panning a landscape composed of the varied roles women played during the war. At the same time, it can be hard to imagine the inner lives of these women, what it felt like to live in constant fear of being discovered, never knowing who to trust, fearing one misstep could be fatal, and how these ideas influenced their decision making in the moment. Mawer's novel takes us into that internal landscape.

The novel follows nineteen-year-old Marian Sutro, British-born but a native French speaker owing to having one French parent. Marian is drafted to carry out an undercover operation in occupied France and parachutes into the country in the middle of the night. The training she received seems paltry in the face of the dangers before her, and she struggles to negotiate her missions and the various personas she assumes. At the same time, she confronts a man from her past who she is tasked with returning to England. Mawer's ethereal prose infuses the story with a haunting cadence that allows the reader to experience the uncertainty and danger of Marian's situation. I found myself holding my breath while reading this absorbing and haunting novel.

The Memory Box by Eva Lesko Natiello

Natiello's psychological thriller is a great example of why readers should give self-published novels a chance. This one hooked me from the start, thanks to Natiello's powerful descriptions. The novel is narrated by Caroline Thompson, a thirty-five year-old mother of two young girls. She has a loving husband, a house in the suburbs, and a memory problem: She can't seem to recall crucial events from her past. A Google search, which she conducts because it's the thing to do among her mom crowd, exposes hidden truths that keep piling up and lead to a finale I did not see coming. Suffice it to say that twists and turns come by the bucketful.

I will tell you that this novel is spine chilling. After I read the last word, I had to sit back for a moment, take a deep breath, and think of cute and comforting things, like kittens, baby hedgehogs, and chocolate bunnies to stop the chills running through me. Part of this is due to the above-mentioned unexpected ending. Natiello leaves it just open-ended enough to allow the reader's imagination to go on whirring after the story on the page ends, but without sacrificing the need to make sense of what happens along the way.

Code Name Verity by Elizabeth Wein

You don't know nothin' about this young adult spy thriller until you finish the book. Which is to say, this novel about two World War II British pilots, Maddie and Queenie, plays with your head in a big way. When the novel opens, Queenie has been captured in occupied France and is being tortured by Nazis. Asked to reveal everything she knows about the British war effort, she agrees to give up all her information and ends up telling a long, winding tale (comparisons to Scheherazade have been made) that includes her friendship with fellow pilot Maddie.

That's all I can tell you about the storyline without spoiling this cunningly plotted book. But I can tell you this: Some fellow readers I've spoken to found the beginning boring only to become subsumed by the story at the halfway point and beyond. Also: Pay attention to everything. Wait, let me say that again: *Pay attention to everything.* No one is to be trusted. Everything is a clue.

CHAPTER 13

Classic and Contemporary British Novels

*"It is only a novel... or, in short,
only some work in which the greatest
powers of the mind are displayed."*

– Jane Austen

As much as it is a real place, the United Kingdom is a place in my imagination cultivated from years of reading British literature. As I shared in Chapter Two, several of the books I fell in love with as a child, the books that made me a reader, were written by British authors and take place in the U.K. Through these stories, it must be admitted, I developed a gilded view of Great Britain, and they are at least partly responsible for why I wanted to spend my college study abroad period there. When the time finally arrived, and I went to study in London, it would have been entirely reasonable for reality to fail to live up to ideal. This has been known to happen, after all. And yet, disappointment and disillusionment did not greet me upon arrival or departure or anywhere in between. What I enjoyed about living in London was the emphasis on order and politeness, but what I adored was the use of humor to diffuse tension and ease uncomfortable or stressful situations.

What I mean by this is perhaps best illustrated by an experience I had on the London Underground during rush hour in a packed train car. When we arrived at one of the stops, a young woman bull-rushed her way to the exit, knocking an older gentleman aside in the process and eliciting more than a few murmurs of disapproval. After the man had recovered his footing, he turned to his friend and said, with a chuckle, "She could play rugby for England, that one." His friend smiled appreciatively, and we rolled on. So illustrative was this moment that I have never forgotten it. The man's witty aside took the sting out of the moment not only for himself but also for everyone in the car who felt offended on his behalf.

This type of humor is kind and gentle. It acknowledges human limitations without being defeated by them, and it allows compassion, instead of anger, to rise up in a moment of frustration. When I'm overwhelmed with nostalgia for my time in the U.K. (which is often), I enjoy visiting it through books that illuminate these aspects of British culture—as well as others I have not experienced myself. For readers interested in experiencing Britain through its literature, the following ten novels offer vivid portraits of everyday life, from Jane Austen's time up to the present.

Northanger Abbey by Jane Austen

Chances are, you have at least a passing familiarity with *Pride and Prejudice*, which has been widely adapted and written about for popular audiences. But when it comes to sparkling romances, I just might prefer *Northanger Abbey*, Austen's hilarious and brilliant spoof of gothic novels. Our heroine is Catherine Morland, the seventeen-year-old daughter of a country clergyman, who is invited to join her wealthier neighbors for the winter season in Bath. Catherine loves to read—you guessed it—gothic novels, and this sets her imagination spinning as she travels with friends and learns hard-won lessons about who to trust.

Wink-wink asides to the reader abound in the novel, including an extended defense of novels themselves, the beginning of which appears in the epigraph to this chapter: *"'What are you reading, Miss--?' 'Oh! It is only a novel!' replies the young lady, while she lays down her book with affected indifference or momentary shame. 'It is only* Cecilia, *or* Camilla, *or* Belinda,*' or, in short, only some work in which the greatest powers of the mind are displayed, in which the most thorough knowledge of human nature, the happiest delineation of its varieties, the liveliest effusions of wit and humor, are conveyed to the world in the best chosen language."*

Great Expectations by **Charles Dickens**

Great Expectations's characters, their struggles, and their strengths could, and do, exist in any age. Switch out the clothes, modes of transportation, and occupations, and the story could take place in 1600 or 2000. The novel opens with young Pip, who lives with his abusive sister and her loving, long-suffering husband Joe, visiting his parents's graves. An escaped convict sets upon him and demands that Pip deliver a metalworking file and food or else the convict's unseen accomplice will do Pip serious damage. What's a young boy to do? Pip complies and thus alters the course of his future, which prompts deep thoughts about the choices we make in the moment and their unexpected and unintended consequences.

The "great expectations" in the title refers to the sudden fortune Pip is offered. Without knowing who his benefactor is, Pip accepts his change of circumstances and leaves his modest village and apprenticeship with Joe to move to London to be schooled in the ways of a proper "gentleman." But what is a proper gentleman? That's the central lesson of the novel, as Pip eventually discovers the hard way. The novel is vivid and beautiful, with comic moments, timeless life lessons, and colorful, unforgettable characters, who are positively Dickensian.

Howards End by E. M. Forster

Three families circle around each other and finally collide in Forster's classic portrait of English society at the turn of the twentieth century. At the head of the posh Wilcox family is Henry, a model of English restraint. Henry's wife Ruth sees much but says little and is relieved not to be burdened by the right to vote. The couple has three children, Charles, Evie, and Paul, who shares a very brief romance with Helen Schlegel, a half-German, half-English orphan. Helen lives with her older, single sister Margaret and their younger brother Tibby, a student at Oxford. The Schlegels have independence and money enough to immerse themselves in cultural activities as well as somewhat bohemian, and at times provocative, interests. At the other end of the socio-economic scale is Leonard Bast, a clerk estranged from his family because of his "unrespectable" wife. The Schlegel sisters befriend Leonard, and the fates of the three families intersect after Henry shares off-hand advice with Margaret and Helen, which they pass on to Leonard, with disastrous consequences.

The novel was written in 1910, with the first World War still a few years in the future but social unrest already beginning to simmer. The characters and events offer a critique of tradition and English society that seems not at all subtle. Forster's characters push against or attempt to fortify limitations imposed at a particular moment in history, within a class system that reinforces gender and socio-economic inequalities. Yet those characters's emotional experiences—frustration, hypocrisy, fear, love—resonate in any time.

The novel's vision of the future feels prophetic, a familiar experience when reading classic novels that so incisively capture the human condition. Forster's brilliance is in seeing the universal in the particular; the minutiae changes, but humans not so much.

Bridget Jones's Diary by Helen Fielding

Bridget Jones's Diary presents the, yes, diary of thirty-something, unlucky-in-love singleton Bridget Jones, in which she keeps track of her weight, her calories, her alcohol intake, and her misadventures in work and relationships. These include dating her boss (Daniel Cleaver), getting dumped by her boss, and changing jobs, which lead to both disasters and successes.

The novel references and borrows aspects of its plot from Austen's *Pride and Prejudice*: Bridget makes a bad first impression on (and of) old family friend Mark Darcy, also the surname of Austen's character. When they first meet as adults at a New Year's Day gathering, Bridget overhears him making unflattering comments about her, as happens in Austen's novel. But, without giving away too much for those who haven't read it, Darcy later saves the day when Bridget's mother gets into a spot of bother with a gentleman "friend."

If you like to laugh and you have not yet read this novel, what are you waiting for? It's jolly good fun!

An Offer You Can't Refuse by Jill Mansell

The cheery mood of Mansell's stories and language are irresistible. Populated by British turns of phrase, idioms, and words that don't exist in American lingo, her writing is so funny and so English, which is to say witty and charming and self-deprecating. I have yet to read a novel of hers that I didn't enjoy, but I have a soft spot for *An Offer You Can't Refuse* because the protagonist, Lola, is a book lover and the manager of a bookshop. If you love to read, reading this novel is a bit like hanging out with a like-minded friend who makes you laugh.

When the book opens, teenaged Lola gets an offer she can't refuse from her boyfriend's posh mum, who offers a fat check in exchange for Lola no longer seeing her son. Fast forward ten years, and the two run into each other again under very different circumstances. As in a Jane Austen novel, a happy ending is guaranteed; the fun is in getting there.

High Fidelity by Nick Hornby

As with Mansell, I would recommend any of Hornby's funny, poignant, and beautifully human novels. You may know *High Fidelity* from the 2000 film adaptation set in Chicago and starring John Cusak. If you've seen it, it won't ruin the book, which has its own tone, mood, and setting (London!).

The novel follows thirty-something record store owner and commitment-phobe Rob Fleming, who has been dumped by his girlfriend Laura. When not engaging in entertaining banter with his quirky employees Dick and Barry, Rob reflects on his past failed relationships and decides to track down his former loves to figure out why his relationships end so badly.

White Teeth by Zadie Smith

In Smith's award-winning debut novel, conflicting beliefs intersect and collide in the cultural mix that is North London during the latter half of the twentieth century.

The story follows two families, the Joneses and the Iqbals, from 1974 to 1999. Working class Archie Jones, who served at the tail end of World War II, makes his living folding paper at a direct mail company. A well meaning if bumbling peacemaker by nature, Archie always carries a coin with him wherever he goes, just in case he needs to make a decision. His twenty-eight-years-younger wife Clara is the daughter of Jamaican immigrants Hortense (a fervent Seventh Day Adventist) and Darcus (a devout couch potato). Archie's best friend is Samad Iqbal, a Bengali Muslim who served alongside Archie during the war. A waiter who longs for more from his life, Samad is fixated on his past, in particular on his great grandfather Mangal Pande, hailed as either freedom fighter or traitor, depending on whom you ask. Samad's arranged marriage to the much younger Alsana produces twin boys, Magid and Millat, born around the same time as Archie and Clara's daughter, Irie.

Shifting perspectives across the decades, the narrative delves into the characters's struggles and temptations—including as immigrants, as Muslims, as non-white citizens of England. In their interlocked stories, intentions and ideals consistently brush up against the messiness of real life: A suicide attempt is foiled by a bad choice of parking spot; a traditional(ish) Muslim wife unwittingly sews S&M costumes as a work-from-home seamstress; a group of righteous religious protesters are stymied by a subway line that is shut down for the day. Ideological battlegrounds coexist with friendship: While Samad bemoans the temptations and dangers of Western life, his best friend is a white Anglican Englishman. Hortense disowns her daughter Clara for marrying Archie, a white man, but since she rather likes this particular white man, she keeps in touch with Archie, yet refuses to speak to her daughter.

It is a marvel of a novel—funny and sad and sprawling—that invites readers to think hard, to empathize with the vastness of human experience, and to be suspicious of drawing any bold, clear lines about who is a friend and who is an enemy.

Longbourn by Jo Baker

Set on the estate that is home to the Bennett family in Jane Austen's *Pride and Prejudice*, *Longbourn* delves into the lives of the servants living below stairs. They include the housekeeper Mrs. Hill and her husband, housemaids Sarah and Polly, and a footman named James, who has a mysterious connection to the estate's residents.

Baker's new take on a familiar landscape is a sensitively rendered portrait of the lives of the servants who move invisibly through *Pride and Prejudice*—their dramas, challenges, and search for love and happiness. Featuring upstairs/downstairs intrigue, made extra-popular with the *Downton Abbey* TV series, *Longbourn* offers readers an opportunity to discover new characters, as well as new perspectives on Austen's beloved ones. The book also explores how class influenced expectations for women *and* men and what coming-of-age looked like for the servant class in the early nineteenth century. Which is to say, the novel provides plenty of great discussion fodder on its own merits.

Lost for Words by Edward St. Aubyn

St. Aubyn's satirical novel is a send-up of a well-known British literary award and revolves around several of the players involved: an author whose publisher accidentally sends the wrong book to the prize committee, a judge mired in scandal, and a writer spurned from the short list and eager for revenge.

The plot can best be described as madcap with an underlying tenderness at its core—especially as regards the characters, whose story-propelling flaws are treated gently. The book is an affectionate if at times ridiculous portrait of those who believe in the power of books. I can only hope St. Aubyn had half as much fun writing it as I had reading it.

44 Scotland Street by Alexander McCall Smith

The first in a series of nine (as of this writing) novels set in Edinburgh, *44 Scotland Street* follows residents of the same building as they work, fall in love, develop friendships, and face disappointments. The residents include a high school graduate on her second gap year, a handsome but arrogant young building surveyor, a middle-aged semi-retired archeologist, and a mother obsessed with turning her little boy into an overachiever.

Interestingly, the novel began its life as a daily serial in *The Scotsman*. This is evidenced in its form: The chapters are short and tightly constructed, with a clear narrative arc that leaves a loose thread to be picked up in the next chapter. Initially, I thought of trying to read it in this way, just one chapter a day. But I didn't have the discipline. I wanted to find out what happens next!

The writing is witty and deeply thoughtful and wise. Not in the least ostentatious, its quiet wisdom has a way of sneaking up on the reader. McCall Smith captures quite accurately how the novel works on the reader in the book's preface, where he writes, *"I think that one can write about amusing subjects and still remain within the realm of serious fiction. It is in observing the minor ways of people that one can still see very clearly the moral dilemmas of our time. One task of fiction is to remind us of the virtues—of love and forgiveness, for example—and these can be portrayed just as well in an ongoing story of everyday life as they can on a more ambitious and more leisurely canvas."*

CHAPTER 14

Novels and Memoirs About the Reading Life

"I declare after all there is no enjoyment like reading!"

– Jane Austen

Reading *A Little Princess* as a child, I connected with Sara Crewe for many reasons, including that she and I were both readers who valued the solace we found through books. This is to say, Sara and I understood each other. Discovering this mutual understanding is one of the pleasures of reading books about the reading life. In addition to exponentially expanding my reading list (gulp), novels and memoirs about readers and reading provide insight into and create a conversation around *how* books have influenced different readers and why. The passionate book lover has his or her own ideas about the how and the why, of course, but experiencing the multiple iterations of reading's value can expand our sense of possibility.

This may explain why these types of book are so exceedingly popular; it's a little bit like having a conversation with a friend who understands us, on at least one level. From a postmodern novel in which the reader is the main character, to memoirs about reading one or more books, to novels that follow the life of a single book and its readers through history, these ten books illuminate both the pleasure of reading and of connecting with fellow readers.

If on a Winter's Night a Traveler by Italo Calvino
Postmodern literature has never been so fun as in Calvino's novel (translated by William Weaver) about a reader trying to read a book called *If on a winter's night a traveler*, which is

written by Italo Calvino, of course. Playful and witty, with a puzzle to solve, the novel's twenty-two chapters alternate between those about "you" reading and the chapters of the novel you're reading. The latter shift and change in style and even content as the novel progresses, often maddeningly breaking off at climactic moments. I should note that in Calvino's world, "you" is a shifty concept as well, which reminds me: There is also a love story.

For a tempting sample, here are the novel's first, delicious sentences: *"You are about to begin reading Italo Calvino's new novel,* If on a winter's night a traveler. *Relax. Concentrate. Dispel every other thought. Let the world around you fade. Best to close the door; the TV is always on in the next room. Tell the others right away, 'No, I don't want to watch TV!' Raise your voice—they won't hear you otherwise [...]."*

People of the Book by Geraldine Brooks

People of the Book offers a fictional account of the Sarajevo Haggadah, a fourteenth-century Passover book featuring illuminations in the style of a Book of Hours, and Hanna Heath, the Australian book conservator hired to restore it. Brooks's novel begins in 1996 with Hanna traveling to Sarajevo to begin her work on the historic text. While examining the book, she extracts artifacts from within its pages—an insect wing, a white hair, and pages with saltwater and wine stains—that might unlock the mystery of the unusual find.

The novel alternates points of view between Hanna's story and the Haggadah's story, with the artifacts providing launching points for explaining why and how the book was created and how it survived across the centuries. Alongside their stories runs Hanna's work on the book as well as her romance with Sarajevo librarian Ozren Karaman, her dysfunctional relationship with her mother (a high-octane surgeon who raised Hanna as a single mother), and a family crisis that reveals an explosive secret about Hanna's parentage. While the novel provides a fascinating study of the meticulous work that book conservators undertake and the endless mysteries books pose as historical artifacts, the story's power lies in Brooks's ability to humanize even the most loathsome figures. She takes readers deep into the lives and hearts of a vast cast of characters, while reminding us of the lives of books.

The Year of Reading Dangerously: How Fifty Great Books (and Two Not-So-Great Ones) Saved My Life by Andy Miller

Miller's lovely memoir is about his experience reading fifty books that he had intended to read at one point in his life and often pretended to have read. Along the way, he revisits his childhood and reflects on how he became a reader, why he lost touch with reading, and, regardless of whether or not he liked them, what he learned from actually reading each of the books on his list from beginning to end.

Though I didn't always agree with Miller's assessments of the books (and in some cases, I had never even heard of them), I loved how he manages to move from hilarious to heartfelt in a beat. I identified with and appreciated his at times unbridled passion for books and reading. I valued the way his discussion prompted to me to reflect on my own reading experiences and that he provides us with potential strategies for reading difficult books. One of the reads Miller struggled with was George Eliot's *Middlemarch*. His wife wisely suggests he "*let the book do the work*," not worry about understanding every line, and read fifty pages a day until he finished. But the more he read, the more the story pulled him in, and he ended up loving it: "*I felt the unmistakable certainty that I had been in the presence of great art, and that my heart had opened in reply.*"

I would call this opening of the heart the best possible outcome of reading a book, and the route Miller took to get to this point offers a lesson that applies not only to reading, but to living: "*[W]hen faced with something we cannot comprehend at once, which was never intended to be snapped up or whizzed through, perhaps 'I didn't like it' is an inadequate response. [...] Instead, perhaps we should have the humility to say: I didn't get it. I need to try harder.*" Hear, hear!

The Eyre Affair by Jasper Fforde

Hard as it is to believe, this wildly inventive and at times hilarious book was Fforde's debut novel. The first in a series about literary detective and war veteran Thursday Next, it's set in a parallel universe: England and Imperial Russia have been fighting the Crimean War for one hundred years, Wales is independent of Great Britain, time travel and cloning are norms, and literature is serious business, at times sparking passions so intense they lead to gang warfare. Oh, and people can travel into the pages of books.

In this first installment, Jane Eyre is kidnapped from the pages of her eponymous novel, and Thursday is called in to investigate. Pulled into the story are one of Thursday's former professors (now a wanted terrorist), a corporation with possibly nefarious intentions, a fellow veteran who Thursday may be in love with, and her father who was once a colonel in the ChronoGuard (the division tasked with ensuring people don't misuse time travel). And a cast of venerable literary characters from classic novels gets up to all sorts of hijinks and drama. The best part about this literary feast is that, as it's the first in a series, the adventures continue beyond the last page.

Tolstoy and the Purple Chair: My Year of Magical Reading by Nina Sankovitch

Sankovitch's heartening memoir was inspired by the year she spent reading a book a day and writing about it on her blog. She undertook the project as a tribute to her sister, who died after a brief illness at the age of forty-six, and as a way to answer for herself why she had been given "*the life card*." In the process, reading became a way of connecting not only to friends and family but also to distant cultures, to the past, and to readers from around the world who found her blog and wrote to her.

In the memoir, talking about the books she read also becomes an occasion for Sankovitch to examine her life and relationships, past and present. Good books, she discovers, illuminate universal human experiences and, through this, connect readers across time, culture, and history. Most significantly, Sankovitch chronicles how her year of reading brought her back to a place of hopefulness about the future.

The Bookman's Tale: A Novel of Obsession by Charlie Lovett

Like Geraldine Brooks's *People of the Book*, Lovett's novel follows a book through the centuries while also telling the story of the contemporary book conservator investigating it. In this case, it's *Pandosto,* a romance Robert Greene penned in 1588 and on which William Shakespeare purportedly based *The Winter's Tale.* The book conservator is Peter Byerly, a recently widowed American antiquarian bookseller. Struggling to cope with the loss of his wife, Peter attempts to re-immerse himself in his passion, finding and selling old books. He travels to England, where the couple had been restoring a cottage and where so much of his work had been based. There, he discovers a Victorian-era portrait of a woman who bears a striking resemblance to his wife. As he investigates its painter, he stumbles onto a centuries-old mystery concerning *Pandosto*, a family rivalry, and a shocking murder.

Told in chapters that alternate between the present and the past, the novel combines literary history, murder mystery, and romance. *The Bookman's Tale* also reminded me that while my backlit e-reader is great for reading on airplanes and in bed, it probably will not be studied by historians in the future.

How Reading Changed My Life by Anna Quindlen

To read Quindlen's memoir about being a lifelong reader is to find a friend between the pages, a fellow traveler through books. Both a novelist and former journalist, Quindlen writes with authority and verve about being bookish. It's a slim volume that can be read in one pleasurable sitting while still tapping into what are, for many readers, core truths and experiences.

As evidence, consider that the book is the source of endlessly quoted and re-quoted *ad infinitum* nuggets of wisdom about the reading life. Just see if you don't recognize this gem: *"Books are the plane, and the train, and the road. They are the destination, and the journey. They are home."*

Mr. Penumbra's 24-Hour Bookstore by Robin Sloan

In Sloan's debut novel, after Clay Jannon loses his job designing logos for a bagel company, he takes a job working the late shift at a twenty-four- hour bookstore whose most requested inventory is books written in a mysterious, indecipherable code. As Clay works to uncover the relationship between his quirky customers and their books, he draws on the resources of his friends, wrestles with the limits of technology, and discovers the nature of immortality.

The novel reads like a delightful mystery, with a cast of imperfect but kind and ethical characters pooling their knowledge and resources and traveling across the country to help Clay discover the secret behind the bookstore's existence. If you like to feel good after you finish the last page of a book, you will probably adore this novel. I think I actually hugged it after I read the last line, and then I wanted to turn back to the beginning and start all over again. Also, it's helpful to know or look up the meaning of the word "penumbra."

Dear Mr. Knightley by Katherine Reay

Books can provide refuge, but they can also become a place to hide from the real world and all its complexities and struggles. This is one of the underlying themes of Reay's epistolary novel. Mr. Knightley isn't the Jane Austen character, and the novel isn't Jane Austen fan fiction of the traditional sort. Rather,

"Mr. Knightley" is the pseudonym of the director of a foundation that gives Samantha Moore, the novel's protagonist, a grant to study journalism. At twenty-three, Sam is an orphan with a troubled past who is trying to find her voice after years spent escaping into books.

She accepts the grant to study at Northwestern University's prestigious Medill School of Journalism, under the condition that she write personal progress letters to Mr. Knightley. He, however, wishes to remain anonymous. The novel is comprised of Sam's letters to him during her course of study as she battles her past and struggles to take control of her life and her story.

Part coming of age and part romance, the novel brims with literary references, which are both a treat and a challenge, as readers try to guess their origins. Kind and gently told, *Dear Mr. Knightley* pays homage to literature while also reminding book lovers to get outside their heads (and books) and live in the messy, scary, complicated world.

The Guernsey and Literary Potato Peel Pie Society by Mary Ann Shaffer and Annie Barrows

This epistolary novel takes place during and after World War II on Britain's Channel Islands, occupied by the Nazis during the war.

Juliet is an author seeking the subject of her next book. Dawsey is a resident of Guernsey (one of the Channel Islands that was occupied) seeking a book recommendation. Finding

Juliet's name and address inscribed on the inside flap of one of his books, Dawsey writes to her. Their correspondence pulls in a diverse, quirky, and loveable cast of characters, many of whom participated in a wartime book group. The titular Society bloomed from a moment of desperation when Nazis discovered a group of residents out and about after curfew. In need of an explanation, they invented the book group then turned it into a reality. The group's experiences during the war and Juliet's experiences writing about them unfold through letters in this sweetly funny and deeply heartwarming novel that explores the power, pleasure, and consolation of reading and community.

CHAPTER 15

Books for Book Lovers

*"When I have a little money, I buy books; and
if I have any left, I buy food and clothes."*

– Desiderius Erasmus

A s illustrated in the anecdote that opens this book, a book can be a calling card: For me, it was bringing *The Goldfinch* on a coffee date that led to a brief but enthusiastic chat about the novel with a perfect stranger. Read books in public—on trains or planes, in coffee shops or waiting rooms—and we get the signal. *What are you reading? How is it? Do you recommend it?*

I have found fellow book lovers just about everywhere I go. And it's the presence of a book in my hand or theirs that can lead to a spontaneous moment of connection, not to mention a book recommendation, exchange of ideas, or a new way of thinking about an old problem.

While the books in Chapter Fourteen explore the ways reading shapes how and who we become, the books in this chapter demonstrate the creative ways that readers have found to celebrate their love of books and the bookish life. In this way, a conversation that may have begun in a single book one or two hundred years ago is picked up, extended, and continued across time and culture, illuminating what endures. These ten books offer fresh perspectives on libraries, the act of reading, literary communities, the creative process, and even what characters might look like when filtered through the visual imagination of an artistic book lover. I found them as inspiring as they are revelatory.

Sorted Books by Nina Katchadourian

Sorted Books fulfills a book lover's insatiable appetite for photographs of books, but with so much more. For twenty years, conceptual artist Katchadourian has entered public and private libraries to sort through their titles, arrange them into found poems, and photograph the results. A poetry-sculpture-photography hybrid, *Sorted Books* documents her work with beautiful photos of artfully arranged books, accompanied by the poems created from their titles and reflections on her process. You don't have to be a poet or poetry enthusiast to appreciate her work or to look at your own collection with fresh eyes.

Katchadourian's results are at times moving, philosophical, revealing, and humorous, and her project has inspired bibliophiles around the world to experiment with her method. Twitter is a great place to discover others's found poems by typing the hashtag #SortedBooks.

Fictitious Dishes: An Album of Literature's Most Memorable Meals by Dinah Fried

Book and foodie cultures meet between the pages of Fried's book, in which she imaginatively recreates and photographs meals from famed novels. *Fictitious Dishes* began as a project Fried undertook while a student at the Rhode Island School of Design. The five meals she conceptualized and photographed as a student blossomed into the fifty that are featured in her book, from a children's picture book (*Blueberries for Sal*) to capital-L-Literature (*Lolita*, *To Kill a Mockingbird*,

A Confederacy of Dunces). Included with the photographs are quotes that inspired her tableaux, along with facts about the food, author, and/or book.

Each photograph is taken from the same overhead perspective, which lends a pleasing uniformity that echoes, for me, in the way books have a standard shape, but each reader shapes what unfolds within. Readers seeking literary analysis won't find it here, at least not in words. Literary interpretation manifests visually, in the intricate settings Fried envisions and creates. The photographs may, however, inspire readers to revisit the works she depicts and read the ones they haven't. They inspired me to add quite a few titles to my to-be-read list.

Among the Janeites: A Journey Through the World of Jane Austen Fandom by Deborah Yaffe

"Janeites" is the term coined for hardcore Austen fans, and Yaffe counts herself among them. For this memoir, Yaffe, a journalist by trade, researched and participated in the myriad ways readers express their passion for Jane Austen. For a year, she immersed herself in everything Austen. In this book, she shares her experiences traveling to Austen landmarks in England, speaking to Austen bloggers (a passionate group, for serious) around the world, and getting fitted for a Regency ball gown (corset included).

It's a fun, if at times bizarre, romp through the Austen fandom subculture, and Yaffe's engaging prose and storytelling entertain while they enlighten. Her book left me marveling at the many ways readers celebrate books and how books can become a catalyst for connection. Austen's novels were written some two hundred years ago, yet they continue to be cherished and remain a conduit through which readers who love them build community.

What We See When We Read by Peter Mendelsund

How refined is our visual sense of the characters we encounter in books? How do words on a page translate into images and expectations in our imaginations? What are we picturing and to what extent do our mental images correspond with the material world? Mendelsund explores these questions and more in his fascinating *What We See When We Read*, an illustrated phenomenology of the act of reading.

The associate art director at Alfred A. Knopf, Mendelsund is responsible for having designed the covers of some six hundred books, including *War and Peace*, *The Metamorphosis*, and *The Girl With the Dragon Tattoo*. The design process manifests the process readers go through in our imaginations as we read: It distills a book's themes, ideas, and characters into representative visual components. Mendelsund brings his design experience, love of literature, and training as a classical pianist to bear on his meditations, with illustrations that support and develop his points. One fascinating example is a picture of Anna Karenina generated using police composite-sketch software.

Though his thoughts dig deep, his tone is playful (and somewhat reminiscent of Marshall McLuhan), conveying a passion for the subject that matches the depth of his insights. This is a delicious and thought- provoking read for those of us who live in books.

Dancing with Mrs. Dalloway: Stories of the Inspiration Behind Great Works of Literature by Celia Johnson

Curious about what inspired great works of literature, Johnson researched the stories behind fifty classic books to uncover the *"sparks of inspiration that prompted great writers to pen their famous works of literature."* Among the featured titles are children's favorites like *Charlotte's Web* and *Winnie the Pooh* and the usual suspects on English class syllabi, among them *The Old Man and the Sea, The Great Gatsby , Pride and Prejudice.*

Her book is divided into six sections, each representing sources from where a writer derived his or her inspiration. For example, "Lightning Strikes" is about writers who stumbled on the germ of an idea while performing *"a mundane task"*—Jules Verne *"flipping through a newspaper,"* Tolstoy settling down for a nap, Robert Louis Stevenson painting a watercolor. "On the Job" covers writers who were inspired by their professions—Gaston Leroux was touring Paris's Palais Garnier opera house while on assignment as a journalist; Dashiell Hammett's novels sprang from his experiences as a private investigator.

Even though Johnson herself acknowledges that the source of a writer's inspiration is much more fluid than her categories suggest, they still reveal how any moment can provide a creative spark, if a writer is open to it. In this way, Johnson's book reminds us to be present in the world. It's good advice for writers and also simply for living.

Well-Read Women: Portraits of Fiction's Most Beloved Heroines by Samantha Hahn

This book is a collection of artist (and reader) Hahn's portraits of fifty of literature's most memorable female characters. In her introduction to the book, Han writes, *"Ultimately, every reader brings his or her own imagination to the task of envisioning these legendary characters. As an artist consumed by the female form, I could not resist the challenge of bringing each of the greatest women in literature (in my own opinion, of course) to life, as, reading intently, I see them spring forth in my mind."*

Alongside her evocative and beautifully stylized watercolors, Hahn features signature quotes from the texts in which the characters appear. For example, with the image of Daisy Buchanan from *The Great Gastby*, Hahn includes the passage, *"All right ... I'm glad it's a girl and I hope she'll be a fool—That's the best thing a girl can be in this world. A beautiful little fool."* Most compelling about *Well-Read Women* is the way it gives detailed form to something we don't typically have access to: what a character looks like in another reader's mind.

84, Charing Cross Road by Helen Hanff

This slim volume is a collection of letters between Hanff and Marks & Co, an antiquarian bookseller in London. Hanff first wrote to the shop in 1949 to request a title. Twenty years of letters, books, and friendship ensued for the New York writer and several of the London bookshop's employees and others connected to them.

Suitable for reading in one sitting, it still packs an emotional wallop, especially when Hanff makes a habit of sending food packages to the English shop employees still suffering the privations of post-war rationing. That's the heartwarming part, but it's also hilarious, as Hanff does her best brash New York-ese to scandalize her proper London counterparts. Perhaps most fascinatingly, *84, Charing Cross Road* harkens back to a time when readers needed more than an Internet connection to access books. And it provides an important reminder to value bookstores and booksellers.

My Ideal Bookshelf, edited by Thessaly La Force, with art by Jane Mount

Book lovers probably won't want to hide this book on a shelf. La Force interviewed one hundred chefs, food writers, cultural figures, fashion designers, musicians, and authors and collected their reflections on the books that have inspired them. To accompany each entry, Mount created compelling original paintings of each contributor's selected titles, rendered in eye-popping colors with hand-lettered book spines.

In addition to being beautiful, *My Ideal Bookshelf* provides insight into the ways books influence and shape their readers. And it inspires us to think about the reads that have influenced and shaped us, along with which ones we would select for our ideal bookshelves.

My Bookstore: Writers Celebrate Their Favorite Places to Browse, Read, and Shop edited by Ronald Rice

Passionate readers tend also to be passionate about where they shop for books. Rice's collection celebrates independent bookstores, the books within them, and the relationship between writers and their favorite shops. Over eighty beloved writers contributed short essays. Each describes his or her independent bookstore, the pivotal one that supported his or her growth and development as a reader.

The essays are beautifully crafted, funny, and moving, and they may quite possibly inspire readers to drive to their nearest indie straightaway. The book begs to be browsed through, just as one might browse through shelves in a bookstore. Each entry includes a black and white sketch of the bookstore under discussion, so it's pretty, too!

The Storied Life of A. J. Fikry by Gabrielle Zevin

Zevin's novel reads like a love letter to reading, books, and booksellers. Set on fictional Alice Island in Massachusetts, the story revolves around loveably bookish A. J. Fikry, a thirty-nine year-old widower with very precise literary tastes, his life and loves, heartbreaks and joys. He provides a model of a twenty-first century bookseller whose life revolves around books and who connects with others through reading. Indeed, those closest to A.J. are a diverse, multi-generational set of readers, writers, and aspiring writers.

The novel touches on a number of key issues that bookish types obsess about—author events, the relationship between memoir and truth, the shift to e-readers, the future of the book business. It concludes on an optimistic note about the latter in a way that feels not only hopeful but true.

CHAPTER 16

Reads for the Fall and Winter Holidays

"What better occupation, really, than to spend the evening at the fireside with a book, with the wind beating on the windows and the lamp burning bright."

– Gustav Flaubert

O ne of my favorite things about living in New England is the four seasons, each of which has its charms. But if I were to pick a favorite, it would have to be the months of September through December. Everything about these months and their holidays enchants me, beginning with the brilliant reds, oranges, and golds of the changing leaves and continuing with pumpkin-flavored everything, turkey with stuffing, fall festivals populated by corn mazes, pumpkin patches, and caramel apples. Even the first frost is welcome when it invites me to curl up with a comfy blanket, in front of a roaring fire, while sipping a gingerbread latte. Add twinkly fairy lights, spiced eggnog, and Nat King Cole crooning in the background to enhance the scene.

All any one of these cozy tableaux requires to complete it is a great read (or ten). In recent years, I have enjoyed synchronizing my literary selections with the holiday being celebrated. If you find yourself of a mind to do likewise, you might enjoy one of these ten stories and novels.

Frankenstein; or, the Modern Prometheus by Mary Shelley (Halloween)

Frankenstein as a massive, green, lumbering dope with giant screws in his neck makes for a Halloween icon. The guy was even a friendly goofball in the 1960s television show *The Munsters*. But the original Frankenstein wasn't a monster, at least not the one you might expect. He was Victor Frankenstein, the protagonist of Mary Shelley's *Frankenstein; or, The Modern Prometheus*, whose subtitle gives you an idea of the book's themes. Frankenstein is so enamored of the natural sciences and so keen on charting new territory that he collects leftover human parts and figures out how to create a living being with them.

But he is so horrified by the being he creates that Frankenstein rejects and flees from the monster, leaving him to fend for himself. Hideously disfigured and continuously spurned by society, the monster turns nasty, and he and Frankenstein end up pursuing each other across Europe. The novel, which can be read as an allegory on multiple levels, is told in three parts—in letters from an explorer (who finds and rescues Frankenstein) to his sister, in first-person narrative by Frankenstein, and in first person narrative by the monster. Neither Frankenstein nor the monster is entirely reliable as a narrator. While both feel they have just cause for their actions, their desires are irreconcilable. Regardless of how right or wrong each is, there is no way for either to win. The novel, one of the first horror stories ever written and still (arguably) one of the best, leaves readers questioning what it means to be human and what it means to be a monster.

Tales of Men and Ghosts by Edith Wharton (Halloween)

Besides being a rather fascinating figure for her time, Wharton is immensely readable and achieved critical and commercial success during her lifetime. Perhaps best known for her novel *The Age of*

Innocence, for which she won the Pulitzer Prize in 1920, Wharton also wrote quite a few supernatural/psychological thriller stories, ten of which are collected in *Tales of Men and Ghosts*. To get into the Halloween spirit, I enjoy dipping into them in October and am always struck by the underlying current of wry humor and emotional tension, along with their straight-up creepy nature.

For example, in "The Bolted Door," Hubert Granice is so disgusted by his inability to get published that he wants to commit suicide. But each time he attempts it, his hands tremble, and he can't go through with it. So he devises a plan to get himself convicted of murder and sentenced to the death penalty, only nothing goes as planned. The story is simultaneously hilarious and chilling.

The Legend of Sleepy Hollow by Washington Irving (Halloween)

Set in a New York Dutch settlement circa 1790 and first published in 1860, *The Legend of Sleepy Hollow* is a charming romp (for a ghost story) through post-Revolutionary New York.

The holiday-appropriate story follows the exploits of the somewhat stuffy and wily schoolteacher Ichabod Crane in his quest to woo the lovely (and wealthy) Katrina Van Tassel. Irving's ghoulish—but not fully terrifying—story and wryly humorous prose combine to create a Halloween story that's more likely to make you smile than to give you nightmares.

SALLY ALLEN

An Old-Fashioned Thanksgiving
by Louisa May Alcott (Thanksgiving)

I confess to having had no idea this short story existed until a few years ago, when I was researching books with a Thanksgiving angle for an article I was writing. Apparently, Alcott's story was also adapted for television and ran on the Hallmark channel in 2008.

The day before Thanksgiving, the very large Bassett family, who live in the hills of New Hampshire, are preparing their holiday meal. But Mr. and Mrs. Bassett are called away unexpectedly to look after a sick grandmother, leaving their older children (of whom there are many) behind to prepare the meal. The children make a few charmingly well-meaning mistakes along the way, but everything comes together nicely in the end. A sweet, heartwarming story, it makes for a great after dinner read-aloud to go with dessert.

The Power of Light: Eight Stories for Hanukkah
by Isaac Bashevis Singer (Hanukkah)

This moving collection of eight short stories, one for each night of Hanukkah, by the Nobel Prize in Literature winner (1978) transports readers through Tsarist Russia, Nazi-occupied Poland, and Brooklyn, NY, among others. Singer deftly weaves history, culture, religion, love, faith, and tradition into these quiet but deeply powerful stories.

I discovered this book at my local library when I was looking for Hanukah children's books to read with my son. Though we don't celebrate Hanukah, many of our friends do, and I wanted my son to understand the holiday's meaning. *The Power of Light* is a beautiful expression of it: Each of the stories revolves around the theme of light overcoming darkness, in ways both literal and figurative.

A Christmas Carol by Charles Dickens (Christmas)

Given the many and varied adaptations, you likely know the story by now, even if you've never read the original. Unable to experience life's ineffable treasures, Ebenezer Scrooge becomes consumed with storing up tangible treasures: work and money. His ensuing rancor and bitterness infect not only him but also those around him, including those who would benefit from his kindness and those who would show him some in return, if he were open to it.

Until one Christmas Eve when he's visited by his deceased business partner, who warns him of the lasting torment that awaits him if he doesn't redirect his life toward the values he has rejected—*"charity, mercy, forebearance, and benevolence."* Though Scrooge wishes to believe the apparition is merely *"a slight disorder of the stomach [...] an undigested bit of beef, a blot of mustard, a crumb of cheese, a fragment of an underdone potato,"* he soon learns otherwise. Journeying to his past, reexamining his present, and glimpsing his future through the ministrations of three ghosts who visit him over the course of the night, Scrooge finally discovers the openness of heart that had eluded him.

The book's story and message are infinitely adaptable. Consider the range of actors who have portrayed the iconic literary character—from Mickey Mouse to Bill Murray to a more orthodox rendition featuring Patrick Stewart. I confess to Murray's *Scrooged* being one of my personal favorite adaptations. But mostly, I love this book, which I have now read at least fifteen times (it's my holiday tradition), and it never gets old and never feels stale.

The Gift of the Magi by O. Henry (Christmas)

This classic, like Dickens's *A Christmas Carol*, has lent itself to adaptations galore. The original 1905 tale tells the story of Jim and Della, a young married couple facing financial difficulty at Christmas. Each longs to buy the perfect present for the other, so both sell their most treasured possessions only to discover ... oh, wait. I don't want to give that part away in case you have not yet read the story. Hint: It's not about the presents. It's about what they signify.

Some fun adaptations of the story include a short film produced for Irish band The Script's song "For the First Time," for which *The Gift of the Magi* provides the plot, and Disney's *Mickey's Once Upon a Christmas* (1999). You have likely seen more than one sitcom riff on the story's theme as well.

The Night Before Christmas
by Nikolai Gogol (Christmas)

Gogol is brilliant at poking fun at human foibles in a way that is paradoxically both biting and affectionate. In this novella, the devil is running amok on Christmas Eve intent on exacting revenge against Vakula, a blacksmith who also paints icons of the devil being defeated. Meanwhile, Vakula is trying to woo the flighty Oksana, whose father is carrying a torch for a village woman, Solokha. Vakula's father is not the only one in love with her, and several other men in the village, including the deacon, converge on Solokha's house on Christmas Eve.

I often laughed out loud while reading Anna Summers's translation of this story, and the ending is just about perfect.

Christmas at Thompson Hall
by Anthony Trollope (Christmas)

Christmas is more prop than plot device in this story about an English couple, the Browns. The couple typically winters in the South of France. At the missus's request, they decide to return to England for a British Christmas at her family's Thompson Hall, where her sister Jane will debut her fiancé.

During a stopover at a hotel in Paris, which is dank and cold and altogether unhelpful to Mr. Brown's heath, Mrs. Brown gets into a spot of bother. Anxious for her husband to feel well enough to travel in the early morning, she decides, in the dark of night, to go in search of mustard from the dining room in order to apply a mustard wrap on his neck. From there, things go very badly indeed, and then they get worse ... and then they go really, really wrong. Each of Mrs. Brown's missteps, set in motion by that infamous sense of British propriety of which you may have heard, leads to another. Trollope spares no detail in describing Mrs. Brown's overwrought inner monologue as contrasted with her comparatively unruffled exterior. I couldn't help myself from gasping and saying, "No!" and then laughing because Trollope is at once sardonic and lavish in his retelling and insightful in his grasp of human motivations and foibles.

Trollope's stories don't quite hold the whole world in them in the way his contemporary Charles Dickens's do. But they are deeply perceptive without being tortured, entertaining while still being instructive, and quite funny. If you enjoy Alexander McCall Smith's books, you might also enjoy Trollope.

My True Love Gave to Me: Twelve Holiday Stories edited by Stephanie Perkins (Winter holidays)

This collection features twelve stories by bestselling young adult writers including Rainbow Rowell, Matt de La Peña, Gayle Forman, Jenny Han, and David Levithan. Each offers some iteration of a love story set during the winter holiday season. "Holiday" is interpreted broadly, encompassing Yule, Hanukah, Christmas, and more. The stories are all impressively luminous. In different ways, each captures some element of the "magic" of the holiday season, some more literally than others. Each story is beautifully written, elegant, and absorbing.

When I read young adult literature, it's usually because I long to remember what it was like for the world to feel *new*. The stories in this collection capture that sense of wonder and possibility. Each one took me to a different place, crafted a different mood, and evoked the feeling from childhood of walking into a familiar room that has been transformed into a magical space, exactly what I associate with the holiday season.

CHAPTER 17

Reconciling with the Inevitable:
We Can't Read All the Books

"Books are not made for furniture,
but there is nothing else that so
beautifully furnishes a house."

– Henry Ward Beecher

I was on a reading roll until I wasn't anymore. Two weeks, four exceptional books, one right after the other, and then ... I hit a wall: I couldn't settle into my next read. I'd pick up a book, read about thirty pages, then my focus would stall, my interest would wane, and I'd drop it. The abandoned books were good books, and maybe, when I return to them (because I'm confident that I will) and read them through to the end, I'll find they are exceptional too. In short, my problem was not the absence of quality books to read. Rather, I believe I was suffering from an experience reminiscent of stuffing myself with a delicious meal and then being unable to look at food for the rest of the day. Before I can enjoy my next meal, I have to allow myself to digest. I was full to bursting with so many good stories, interesting characters, compelling narrative voices, thought-provoking scenarios, that I couldn't take in any more. It was time for a break.

And yet ... I don't know quite what to do with myself when I don't have a book I'm into, and worse, there are so many books I have not yet read. And they keep accumulating. My inner voice shrieks, *There is no time for breaks!* How to deal with the anxiety about all the unread books? Especially in the face of ubiquitous articles with titles like, "Seven Must-Read Books Coming Out in April" or "Books to Watch for this Fall" or "Three Hundred and Thirty-Three Books You Must Read Immediately That Were Published Yesterday. Hurry, Fool!" Or even this book, with its lists of reads *I* recommend?

When I begin thinking about all the books that have been written, are being written right now, and will be written in the immediate and long-term future, just like that, I'm imaginatively transported into one of those cartoons where a field of corn explodes, burying me under a mountain of popcorn. Except instead of a field of corn, it's a field of writers hacking away on their computers, and instead of popcorn proliferating on the landscape, it's books. And all I can think is, *I will never catch up!* And this is where it ends. Because *of course* I won't catch up. It is impossible to catch up. Best to accept that I can't read every book ever written, even the deeply eloquent and interesting ones. I mean, this is obvious, right?

Still, it's one thing to reconcile ourselves with an unpleasant reality intellectually and quite another to reconcile ourselves emotionally. I still don't know that I *have* reconciled myself, if I'm honest. Where I have found comfort is in remembering that meaningful choices and what I do with the books I read matter more than racing toward a finish line, reading as much as I can, as fast as I can. Instead of the mountain of exploding popcorn, I focus on the idea that everything recurs.

In his novel *The Unbearable Lightness of Being,* Milan Kundera explores how eternal recurrence may feel like a burden. We can reconcile ourselves with things that are transitory because—and I love how Kundera puts this—*"in the sunset of dissolution, everything is illuminated by the aura of nostalgia."* It may be harder to reconcile ourselves with events that forever recur and thus are forever in motion, which is a bit like trying to chase a ball down a hill. I will never catch the ball, which is to say: I will never read all the books. But keeping in mind the idea of meaningful choices, I think of the eternal return as it's rendered in *Groundhog Day*, in which Bill Murray's character has to relive the same day over and over until he achieves "enlightenment" (and gets the girl). To apply this to the reading problem, it's not necessary to read everything that's coming out right now or that has ever been written. It's not necessary to jump into a new book the moment we finish the last one. It's not necessary to read *all the books*, but to read the books that help move us toward some sort of personal enlightenment that—because it's so hard won—moves us towards greater understanding of ourselves and greater empathy for the (eternally recurring) human struggle.

When overwhelm begins to set in, when the critics tell me about the books I *should* read, and I forget this big picture ideal, I try to return to that quiet place in my imagination that knows, deeply and intuitively, how reading books of all kinds has enriched my life. I try to be patient, to remember that being a reader is more than gobbling all the books, inhaling them one after the other like a bookish Ms. Pacman. It's about more than reading the right or best books according to someone I've never met.

Being a reader is about taking the time to have a conversation with a book, to give it my devoted time and attention, to value the efforts of its creator, to seek connection with others who have engaged in this same conversation. As the years pass, I learn more and more to value these communal experiences of being a reader as much as I do the solitary act of reading itself. And when I finish a great (or good) book, when I find myself full to bursting, I remember that my reading life is enriched by any number of experiences besides reading the next or the newest or the best book.

I've collected fifteen of those favorite experiences, presented in no particular order of favorite-ness. Should you find yourself stuck, overwhelmed, and/or otherwise struggling to read, I hope one or more of these may prove helpful to you.

Rereading favorite parts of a recently finished book. I'm learning not to fight it when I'm not ready to move on to a new book because the last one was so wonderful. Instead, I allow myself to linger with that book and extend my experience with it. After I read *All the Light We Cannot See* by Anthony Doerr, which was densely layered and moved back and forth through time quite a bit, I realized that my sense of the story's chronology was somewhat tenuous. Instead of starting a new book, which I didn't feel ready for, I went back to the beginning and reread the first three chapters. They looked quite different at the end of the story than they had at the beginning. I also reread my notes and highlights, seeing how the pieces fit together and relishing a little more time with the characters I had grown to love.

Taking a day off of reading. As I previously mentioned, I tend to feel a little discombobulated when I'm not reading a book. Reading is how I take productive breaks from work and how I like to begin and end each day. But it's not such a terrible thing to spend a day with my thoughts, especially my thoughts about a good book I just finished. It's quite fun, actually, to carry the characters around with me, daydream about and moon over them, stare at the book cover, read others's reviews, or join an online or drop-in library discussion about the book. Also, even if one is not a writer, taking some time to record one's thoughts about a book ensures that, years hence, if memory fails, a reference remains. Things I like to keep track of include:

* Author's name, number of pages, genre, subject, and what form I read the book in (hardcover, paper, e-book)
* How I discovered or acquired the book
* Where and when I read it
* Noteworthy experiences, intellectual or emotional, I had while reading the book
* The book's basic plot, setting, main characters, point of view
* My favorite lines or quotes
* Whether I would recommend the book and for whom I would recommend it.

Reading, watching, or listening to author interviews. When I enjoy or otherwise value a book, I become curious about the person who created it. Some readers will plunge into another book by the same author straightaway; I tend to think this can be tricky, since expectations have been set that can be hard to meet. But the Internet offers an abundance of options for getting to know authors, including on their and/or their publishers's websites. If the author spoke at a local library or bookstore, their websites may carry podcasts or videos of the author's talk, and of course, YouTube offers a wealth of resources. Applying this as a practice, I was thrilled to discover a video of Doerr, posted on his publisher's website, explaining how he came up with the idea for *All the Light We Cannot See*. These are the next best option to attending an author talk. And speaking of...

Attending author talks. I'm fascinated by the creative process and love to watch people make things. For the most part, you can't watch authors write books. At least, not in the sense that you can crawl inside their heads and see how random, everyday events—reading a news report, seeing a parade float almost crash into a car, overhearing a conversation—somehow blossomed into fully fleshed worlds, with their own characters and consequences and internal logic. Being in the same room with authors as they share their stories of inspiration and process and having the opportunity to ask them questions are as close as we can come. I've discovered more great reads than I can count by attending author talks. Unlike, say, going to the movies, they are usually free at your local library or bookstore, and they are a great way to support authors.

Reading (parts of) a book referenced in the book you just read. Great books often reference other great books.

These references spark my curiosity. I wonder how reading a book that my favorite characters have also read might deepen my connection to and understanding of them. After finishing *All the Light We Cannot See*, in which Jules Verne's *20,000 Leagues Under the Sea* figures prominently, it occurred to me that, somewhat shockingly, I could not recall ever having read any of Verne's novels. But I happened to have a lovely edition of *20,000 Leagues* on my bookshelf. It's a great book all on its own, but reading it also helped me feel closer to Marie-Laure, Doerr's protagonist who reads Verne's novel at several seminal moments in her story.

Rereading a beloved childhood favorite. Rereading childhood favorites tends to remind me of why I grew to love books and reading in the first place. So when I feel unsure of what to read next or find myself wondering if my next read can possibly satisfy as much as my previous one did, I return to those books that first nurtured my love of reading. Recently, I discovered that the entire *All-of-a-Kind Family* series is available on my e-reader and downloaded the lot of them. With their episodic chapters, the series is great for reading in bits and pieces, though once I begin, I tend to want to read the whole book from beginning to end.

Reading a book about books. It would seem self-serving to bring this up, given the nature of this book, but since you're already here ... What I love about reading these kinds of books is the kinship, the lovely feeling of meeting another book lover on the page. The options can be staggering (as you may have

SALLY ALLEN

gathered from Chapters Fourteen and Fifteen)—memoirs about reading, memoirs about reading a particular book, series or author, nonfiction about the making of books, novels set in bookstores, nonfiction books by artists. And obviously, these books overflow with suggestions for what to read next.

Taking an idle stroll through a bookstore or library. I tend to head straight for the "staff recommendations" section, which works especially well when I have a relationship with said staff. But even if I don't, walking around without intention, picking books up randomly and reading author blurbs can be illuminating, and I have discovered many a great book this way. And while you're at the bookstore…

Judging a book by its cover. But only for the purposes of experimentation! Driven by my preoccupations, I tend to get stuck on the same genres, the same themes, ideas, and questions, the same trusted authors. One way I challenge myself is by allowing myself to be drawn to an arresting book cover. This is how I discovered Jill Mansell's romantic comedies: The cover of one of her books caught my eye as I was wandering through the fiction section at my local library's annual book sale. Even though I'm not a prolific reader of romance novels, the fun and funny twists and turns her stories take, and her loveable, self-deprecating characters won me over. Now, I consider Mansell one of my go-to writers when I need a bit of cheering up.

Downloading free samples. One of my (many) favorite things about e-readers is the free samples, which usually mean at least a chapter and sometimes more. When I see or hear about an interesting book, I download, if available, the free sample. It helps me keep track of books I'm looking forward to reading in one place. When I feel stuck choosing what to read next, they are right there waiting to be discovered, whether I read them digitally or head to my favorite brick-and-mortar bookstore for a paper copy. Even if you don't have a Nook, Kindle, or Kobo, if you have a smartphone, computer, or tablet, you have an e-reader. And that means access to free samples—just like in the grocery store, but better because it's books!

Switching up the genre. When I recently found myself struggling to decide what to read next, I realized the books I'd been reading were on the "heavy" side—literally and figuratively. They were very long books while also being richly imagined, emotionally and philosophically deep, and somewhat mournful. I needed something different in mood and tone, which is how I discovered Helen Fielding's *Bridget Jones's Diary*. It's the kind of book that feels like hanging out with a fun friend who will make me laugh out loud and remind me that it can also feel good to laugh at myself, which turned out to be just what I needed at that moment.

Reading poetry. And speaking of new genres … despite my deep faith in literature to prompt empathy and insight, poetry and I have never been the closest of confidantes. I have taken to thinking of poetry as I would an acquaintance admired from afar, that one inscrutable person who, when you speak with her or hear what he's been doing, impresses you. But somehow, you can never get past the surface pleasantries when in that person's presence. I may never feel as comfortable reading poetry as I do prose, possibly because poetry does not "mean" in the same way that narrative does. But reading *Eugene Onegin* taught me to open myself to storytelling grounded in image and emotion and to appreciate poetry for its ability to awaken the senses through these. Reading poetry also reminds me to be humble in the face of the unknown, instead of trying to reduce or dismiss it.

Reading a classic. Classics, Italo Calvino tells us, are so because they *"never finished saying what [they have] to say."* This is not to say that we shouldn't read contemporary literature. But it can be a relief to step off the spinning carousel of the newest and latest and spend time with a book that has been generating conversations for decades, centuries, or longer.

Creating and contributing to little free libraries. These mini lending libraries are popping up in unexpected places as a way for book lovers to share and spread their love of books and reading. The concept is simple and simply wonderful: Create a structure that can house books, install it in an approved public space, and invite readers to exchange one of their books for one of yours. Among the many advantages of little free libraries: They are a great way to recycle books, share those you love, and promote community engagement through reading. In 2014, I installed one at one of my favorite local coffee shops, and I love popping in to see which books have been taken and which have been left, and providing a fresh supply of books I'm exited to share with other readers. Readers interested in starting their own little free libraries can find more information and resources at LittleFreeLibrary.org.

Trying a bookish project. I will admit that I shudder at the thought of crafting with books themselves, but not all bookish projects involve the cutting up of books: Transforming stair treads into a hand-painted bookshelf, crafting a case for an e-reader, engaging in a poetry and/or photography project like Nina Katchadourian's *Sorted Books* or Dinah Fried's *Fictitious Dishes* are all inspired ideas for expressing love of books and reading. And they just might inspire your next read.

CHAPTER 18

The Reader and Her Book

"There is no scent so pleasant to my nostrils as that faint, subtle reek which comes from an ancient book."

– Arthur Conan Doyle

I 've never been very good with endings, especially with books ending. Melancholy descends as I contemplate leaving the world of the story behind. This applies not only to reading books but to writing them as well. I can only hope you have found a fraction of the pleasure reading this and discovering the books within it as I have enjoyed writing it and reading them. Before I leave you to pursue your next reading adventure, I want to share a final anecdote, one that may ring familiar.

"Why do you have a book in your bag?" My nine-year-old niece asked me this on a summer Sunday afternoon during an impromptu inspection of my bulbous handbag. My family had convened in the wilds of Connecticut to greet my thirteen-year-old nephew upon his completion of a week of sleep-away camp. We are a small tribe but committed to the grand gesture. So those of us who could make it met at the campgrounds on Bantam Lake to form the welcoming committee, arriving from our various corners of New York and New England.

Following the flurry of strategic planning phone calls came the swatting of mosquitoes, the sipping of ice cold water from little plastic cups, the inspection of the digs, more ineffectual batting at mosquitoes (oh, the mosquitoes!). We then engaged in a spirited round of musical cars so the boys could ride together. Finally, our three-car motorcade rolled out in search of vittles and air conditioning, and we settled into a very picturesque bistro.

During lunch, my approximately three-ton handbag and I had been doing our best Mary Poppins-and-her-carpetbag impression for my niece, who marveled at my ability to meet her every request. Pen? Check. Games? Check (a deck of cards). I also produced a notebook, lip balm, and a clever contraption that allows me to hang my handbag from any flat surface. That last item made quite the impression. But it was the book that seemed most unexpected to her.

"I always carry a book," I said.

There really is no explanation. I mean, at what point, exactly, had I been thinking I could pull out my book and read? While driving? While strolling the campgrounds? While dining with four adults and three children in a restaurant? But still. I can never resist bringing a book with me. Of all the "essential" items I'm likely to leave behind when rushing from my home—my mobile, my wallet, even my keys—I cannot recall ever forgetting to bring a book. *Just in case.*

BIBLIOGRAPHY

In numerous instances, I quote authors directly from these editions in order to demonstrate the brilliance of the language and/or because I could not improve upon the wording. My (not-so-secret) intention is for these quoted passages to inspire readers to acquire and enjoy these books in their entirety. Any errors in transcription are my own.

Abbott, Megan E. *The End of Everything: A Novel.* Little, Brown, 2011.

Aciman, André. *Harvard Square: A Novel.* W. W. Norton, 2013.

Alcott, Louisa May. *Little Women.* Oxford UP, 1979.

Alcott, Louisa May. *An Old-fashioned Thanksgiving.* CreateSpace, 2014.

Alexie, Sherman. *The Absolutely True Diary of a Part-time Indian.* Little, Brown Books for Young Readers: 2007.

Adichie, Chimamanda Ngozi. *Americanah: A Novel.* Knopf, 2013.

Allen, Sarah Addison. *The Girl Who Chased the Moon: A Novel.* Bantam, 2010.

Asher, Jay, and Carolyn Mackler. *The Future of Us.* Razorbill, 2011.

Atkinson, Kate. *Life after Life: A Novel.* Reagan Arthur, 2013.

Aubyn, Edward St. *Lost for Words: A Novel.* Farrar, Straus and Giroux, 2014.

Austen, Jane. *Northanger Abbey.* Barnes & Noble Classics, 2007.

Baker, Jo. *Longbourn.* Alfred A. Knopf, 2013.

Batuman, Elif. *The Possessed: Adventures with Russian Books and the People Who Read Them.* Farrar, Straus and Giroux, 2010.

Benioff, David. *City of Thieves: A Novel.* Viking, 2008.

Bertino, Marie-Helene. *2 A.M. at The Cat's Pajamas: A Novel.* Crown, 2014.

Bloom, Amy. *Lucky Us: A Novel.* Random House, 2014.

2sUyti

Blume, Judy. *Starring Sally J. Freedman as Herself.* Bradbury, 1977.

Bond, Michael, and Peggy Fortnum. *A Bear Called Paddington.* Dell, 1970.

Bradbury, Ray. *Fahrenheit 451.* Simon and Schuster, 1967.

Bremzen, Anya Von. *Mastering the Art of Soviet Cooking: A Memoir of Food and Longing.* Crown, 2013.

Brooks, Geraldine. *People of the Book: A Novel.* Penguin, 2008.

Brooks, Max. *World War Z: An Oral History of the Zombie War.* Crown, 2006.

Bulgakov, Mikhail, and Mirra Ginsburg. *The Master and Margarita.* Grove, 1994.

Bulgakov, Mikhail, Richard Pevear, and Larissa Volokhonsky. *The Master and Margarita.* Penguin Classics, 2001.

Burnett, Frances Hodgson. *A Little Princess.* Lippincott, 1963.

Butler, Octavia E. *Kindred.* Beacon, 1988.

Byrd, Max. *The Paris Deadline: A Novel.* Turner, 2012.

Calvino, Italo, and William Weaver. *If on a Winter's Night a Traveler.* Harcourt Brace Jovanovich, 1982.

Calvino, Italo. *Why Read the Classics?* Knopf Canada, 2001.

Carré, John Le. *The Spy Who Came in from the Cold.* Coward-McCann, 1964.

Chabon, Michael. *Wonder Boys.* Villard, 1995.

Collins, Suzanne. *The Hunger Games.* Scholastic, 2008.

Davis, Tanita S. *Mare's War.* Alfred A. Knopf, 2009.

Deresiewicz, William. *A Jane Austen Education: How Six Novels Taught Me about Love, Friendship, and the Things That Really Matter.* Penguin, 2011.

Dickens, Charles. *Great Expectations.* Penguin Classics, 2002.

Dickens, Charles. *A Christmas Carol.* Candlewick, 2006.

Doerr, Anthony. *All the Light We Cannot See: A Novel.* Scribner, 2014.

Dolan, Lian. *Elizabeth the First Wife.* Prospect Park, 2013.

Eberts, Marjorie, and Margaret Gisler. *Careers for Bookworms & Other Literary Types.* VGM Career Horizons, 1990.

Eberts, Marjorie, and Margaret Gisler. *McGraw-Hill's Careers for Bookworms & Other Literary Types.* McGraw-Hill, 2009.

Eugenides, Jeffrey. *The Marriage Plot.* Farrar, Straus and Giroux, 2011.

Farris, Joseph. *A Soldier's Sketchbook: From the Front Lines of World War II.* National Geographic, 2011.

Fforde, Jasper. *The Eyre Affair: A Novel.* Penguin, 2003.

Fielding, Helen. *Bridget Jones's Diary: A Novel.* Penguin, 2010.

Fielding, Henry. *The History of Tom Jones, a Foundling.* Penguin Classics, Reprint Edition, 2005.

Finn, Peter, and Petra Couvée. *The Zhivago Affair: The Kremlin, the CIA, and the Battle over a Forbidden Book.* Pantheon, 2014.

Flaubert, Gustave, and Francis Steegmuller. *Madame Bovary.* Random House, 1957.

Follett, Ken. *The Man from St. Petersburg.* NAL, 2003.

Forster, E. M. *Howards End.* Penguin Classics, 2000.

Fowler, Karen Joy. *We Are All Completely Beside Ourselves.* Marian Wood/Putnam, 2013.

Freedman, Colette. *The Affair.* Kensington, 2013.

Fried, Dinah. *Fictitious Dishes: An Album of Literature's Most Memorable Meals.* Harper Design, 2014.

Furst, Alan. *Mission to Paris: A Novel.* Random House, 2012.

Gaiman, Neil. *American Gods: The Tenth Anniversary Edition.* William Morrow &, 2012.

Galloway, Steven. *The Cellist of Sarajevo.* Riverhead, 2008.

Gopnik, Adam. *Paris to the Moon.* Random House, 2000.

Goulish, Matthew. *39 Microlectures: In Proximity of Performance.* Routledge, 2000.

Greer, Andrew Sean. *The Impossible Lives of Greta Wells.* Ecco, 2013.

Hahn, Samantha. *Well-read Women: Portraits of Fiction's Most Beloved Heroines.* Chronicle, 2013.

Hanff, Helene. *84, Charing Cross Road.* Avon, 1974.

Hannah, Kristin. *Winter Garden.* St. Martin's, 2010.

Hayes, Suzanne, and Loretta Nyhan. *I'll Be Seeing You.* Harlequin MIRA, 2013.

Hemingway, Ernest. *A Farewell to Arms, The Hemingway Library Edition.* Scribner Classics, 2012.

Henry, O. *The Gift of the Magi.* Candlewick, 2008.

Hoffman, Alice. *The Museum of Extraordinary Things: A Novel.* Scribner, 2014.

Holt, Elliott. *You Are One of Them.* Penguin, 2013.

Hornby, Nick. *High Fidelity.* Riverhaed Trade, 1996.

Howe, Katherine. *The Physick Book of Deliverance Dane: A Novel.* Hyperion, 2009.

Hutchins, Scott. *A Working Theory of Love.* Penguin, 2012.

Irving, Washington. *The Legend of Sleepy Hollow.* Penguin Group, 2014.

Iyer, Lars. *Wittgenstein Jr.* Melville House, 2014.

Johnson, Celia Blue. *Dancing with Mrs. Dalloway: Stories of the Inspiration behind Great Works of Literature.* Perigee, 2011.

Joyce, Rachel. *The Unlikely Pilgrimage of Harold Fry: A Novel.* Random House, 2012.

Katchadourian, Nina. *Sorted Books.* Chronicle Books, 2013.

Kerouac, Jack. *On the Road.* Viking, 1997.

Kerouac, Jack. *Satori in Paris; And, Pic: Two Novels.* Grove, 1988.

Konigsburg, E. L. *From the Mixed-Up Files of Mrs. Basil E. Fankweiler.* Atheneum Books for Young Readers; Reprint edition, 2007.

Kundera, Milan. *The Unbearable Lightness of Being.* HarperCollins, 1999.

Lahiri, Jhumpa. *The Lowland: A Novel.* Knopf Doubleday, 2013.

Lancaster, Jen. *Here I Go Again.* New American Library, 2013.

Lang, Maya. *The Sixteenth of June: A Novel.* Scribner, 2014.

Larsen, Nella. *Passing.* Penguin, 1997.

Liebert, Emily. *You Knew Me When.* Penguin, 2013.

Locke, Attica. *The Cutting Season.* HarperCollins, 2012.

Lockhart, E. *We Were Liars.* Delacorte, 2014.

Lovett, Charles C. *The Bookman's Tale: A Novel of Obsession.* Penguin Group, 2013.

Lowry, Lois. *The Giver.* Houghton Mifflin, 1993.

Malouf, David. *Ransom.* Pantheon, 2010.

Mansell, Jill. *An Offer You Can't Refuse.* Source Landmark, 2009.

Martin, Steve. *Shopgirl.* Hyperion, 2000.

Mawer, Simon. *Trapeze*. Other, 2012.

McBride, James. *The Good Lord Bird*. Riverhead, 2013.

Mead, Rebecca. *My Life in Middlemarch*. Crown, 2014.

Mendelsund, Peter. *What We See When We Read*. Vintage, 2014.

Miller, Andy. *The Year of Reading Dangerously: How Fifty Great Books (and Two Not-so-great Ones) Saved My Life*. Harper Perennial, 2014.

Miller, Madeline. *The Song of Achilles*. Ecco, 2012.

Morgenstern, Erin. *The Night Circus: A Novel*. Doubleday, 2011.

Moriarty, Liane. *The Husband's Secret*. G. P. Putnam's Sons, 2013

Mount, Jane, and Thessaly La Force. *My Ideal Bookshelf*. Little, Brown, 2012.

Murakami, Haruki, Philip Gabriel, and Jay Rubin. *IQ84*. Alfred A. Knopf, 2011.

Nabokov, Vladimir. *Pnin*. Vintage, 1989.

Natiello, Eva Lesko. *The Memory Box*. Fine Line, 2014.

Niffenegger, Audrey. *The Time Traveler's Wife: A Novel*. MacAdam/Cage, 2003.

North, Claire. *The First Fifteen Lives of Harry August*. Redhook, 2014.

O'Brien, Tim. *The Things They Carried, 20 Anv Edition*. Houghton Mifflin Harcourt, 2010.

Oliver, Lauren. *Before I Fall*. HarperCollins, 2010.

Ormondroyd, Edward, and Peggie Bach. *Time at the Top*. Parnassus, 1963.

Otsuka, Julie. *The Buddha in the Attic*. Alfred A. Knopf, 2011.

Oyeyemi, Helen. *Boy, Snow, Bird: A Novel*. Riverhead, 2014.

Palma, Félix J., and Nick Caistor. *The Map of Time: A Novel*. Atria, 2011.

Pasternak, Boris Leonidovich, Richard Pevear, and Larissa Volokhonsky. *Doctor Zhivago*. Pantheon, 2010.

Perkins, Stephanie. *My True Love Gave to Me: Twelve Holiday Stories*. St. Martin's Griffin, 2014.

Perrotta, Tom. *Little Children*. St. Martin's, 2004.

Prince, Cathryn J. *Death in the Baltic: The Sinking of the Wilhelm Gustloff*. Palgrave Macmillan Trade, 2013.

Pushkin, Aleksandr Sergeevich, and James E. Falen. *Eugene Onegin*. Oxford UP, 1995.

Quick, Matthew. *The Good Luck of Right Now: A Novel*. Harper, 2014.

Quindlen, Anna. *How Reading Changed My Life*. Ballantine, 1998.

Rachman, Tom. *The Imperfectionists: A Novel*. Random House, 2010.

Reay, Katherine. *Dear Mr. Knightley: A Novel*. Thomas Nelson, 2013.

Rice, Ronald. *My Bookstore: Writers Celebrate Their Favorite Places to Browse, Read, and Shop*. Black Dog & Leventhal, 2012.

Rodgers, Mary. *Freaky Friday*. Harper & Row, 1972.

Rodgers, Nile. *Le Freak: An Upside down Story of Family, Disco, and Destiny*. Spiegel & Grau, 2011.

Rogan, Charlotte. *The Lifeboat: A Novel*. Little, Brown, 2012.

Rowell, Rainbow. *Landline*. St. Martin's, 2014.

Saint-Exupéry, Antoine De, and Katherine Woods. *The Little Prince*. Harcourt, Brace & World, 1943.

Sankovitch, Nina. *Tolstoy and the Purple Chair: My Year of Magical Reading*. Harper, 2011.

Schneider, Robyn. *The Beginning of Everything*. HarperCollins, 2013.

Schulman, Helen. *This Beautiful Life: A Novel*. HarperCollins, 2011.

Schumacher, Julie. *Dear Committee Members*. Knopf Doubleday, 2014.

Selznick, Brian. *The Invention of Hugo Cabret: A Novel in Words and Pictures*. Scholastic, 2007.

Semple, Maria. *Where'd You Go, Bernadette: A Novel*. Little, Brown, 2012

Shaffer, Mary Ann., and Annie Barrows. *The Guernsey Literary and Potato Peel Pie Society*. Random House, 2009.

Shelley, Mary Wollstonecraft. *Frankenstein, Or, The Modern Prometheus*. Dover Publications, 1994.

Sholokhov, Mikhail Aleksandrovich, and Stephen Garry. *And Quiet Flows the Don*. Knopf Doubleday, 1989.

Singer, Isaac Bashevis. *The Power of Light: Eight Stories for Hanukkah*. Farrar, Straus, Giroux, 1990.

Sloan, Robin. *Mr. Penumbra's 24-hour Bookstore*. Farrar, Straus and Giroux, 2012.

Smith, Alexander McCall. *44 Scotland Street*. Knopf Doubleday Publishing Group, 2005.

Smith, Jennifer E. *The Statistical Probability of Love at First Sight*. Little, Brown, 2012.

Smith, Zadie. *White Teeth: A Novel*. Knopf Doubleday, 2001.

Stedman, M. L. *The Light Between Oceans: A Novel*. Scribner, 2012.

Straub, Emma. *The Vacationers*. Riverhead, 2014.

Strayed, Cheryl. *Wild: From Lost to Found on the Pacific Crest Trail*. Knopf Doubleday, 2012.

Tarshis, Lauren, and Scott Dawson. *I Survived the Battle of Gettysburg, 1863*. Scholastic, 2013.

Tartt, Donna. *The Goldfinch*. Little, Brown, 2014.

Taylor, Sydney. *All-of-a-kind Family*. Wilcox and Follett, 1951.

Thomas, Amy. *Paris, My Sweet: A Year in the City of Light (and Dark Chocolate)*. Source, 2012.

Travers, P. L., and Mary Shepard. *Mary Poppins*. Harcourt, Brace & World, 1962.

Tropper, Jonathan. *This Is Where I Leave You*. Penguin Publishing Group, 2009.

Urbach, Linda. *Madame Bovary's Daughter: A Novel*. Bantam Trade Paperbacks, 2011.

Verne, Jules. *Twenty Thousand Leagues under the Sea*. Barnes & Noble, 2012.

Waldman, Adelle. *The Love Affairs of Nathaniel P.: A Novel*. Henry Holt, 2013.

Wein, Elizabeth. *Code Name Verity*. Hyperion, 2012.

Wells, H. G. *The Time Machine*. Floating, 2008.

West, James L. III. Conversations with William Styron. University Press of Mississippi, 1985.

Wharton, Edith. *Ethan Frome*. Signet Classic, 2009.

Wharton, Edith. *Tales of Men and Ghosts*. Barnes & Noble Digital Library, 2011.

White, E. B., and Garth Williams. *Charlotte's Web*. Harper Collins, 2012.

Woodruff, Lee. *Those We Love Most*. Hyperion, 2012.

Woodson, Jacqueline. *Hush*. Penguin Young Readers Group, 2002.

Yaffe, Deborah. *Among the Janeites: A Journey through the World of Jane Austen Fandom*. Houghton, Mifflin, Harcourt, 2013.

Zevin, Gabrielle. *The Storied Life of A.J. Fikry: A Novel*. Algonquin, 2014.

ACKNOWLEDGEMENTS

Like reading, writing is both solitary and communal. This book would not exist without the opportunities, encouragement, and support provided by so many people I'm lucky to have in my life, and some who I've never met.

Most obviously, this book would not exist without the authors who wrote the books that have transported me and inspired me to think and write. Thank you for the books!

So many, many huzzahs to my dear and terrifyingly brilliant friend and editor Stephanie Hopkins. If parallel lives exist, an alternate me who never met the divine Ms. Hopkins probably doesn't understand why she feels a huge gap in her life. And if past lives exist, I'm pretty sure I've been following Stephanie around for millennia.

This book would not be what it is without my supremely talented friend and editor Alysa Salzberg, who understood this project from the start. Alysa is like the best kind of personal trainer: You don't realize how hard she's pushing you because you're having so much fun in the process.

I am so lucky to know my friend, reading twin, and Books, Ink contributing editor Jessica Collins, who is a constant source of inspiration, great book recommendations, and fascinating conversation. Plus, I always know what answer I'll get on a BuzzFeed literary quiz because it's usually whatever Jessica got.

I am so grateful for HamletHub's exuberant founder, Kerry Anne Ducey, who provided me with a platform to write about and build community around what I love. This book began on Books, Ink at HamletHub.

I am also grateful for challenging and fun assignments from Marcelle Soviero, editor-in-chief of *Brain, Child: The Magazine for Thinking Mothers*, who is as warm-hearted as she is gifted at her craft. Several of the discussions in this book appeared in a different form in print and/or online editions of *Brain, Child: The Magazine for Thinking Mothers* .

A special thank you to Anthony Karge, the wonderfully talented (and funny) editor who assigned me my first non-academic book piece.

I also want to thank:

Early readers Carolyn Hopkins and Ginny Benson for their close readings and invaluable feedback.

My fabulous, best book group ever—Heather, Ashley, Tracy, Chris, and Grace—for the great conversations, debates, and ever-expanding to-be-read list.

My equally fabulous writer's group—Jessica, Heather, and Mimi—for your insights, sensitivity, kindness, and quiet brilliance.

And of course, I am most thankful for my beautiful family, who are at the center of everything that matters most to me.

ABOUT THE AUTHOR

Sally Allen is an award-winning writer and teacher. She holds a Ph.D. from New York University in English Education, with an emphasis in writing and rhetoric, and a M.A. in English Language and Literature. She has taught writing, literature, and communications at New York University, Fairfield University, Sacred Heart University, and Post University, and consulted in the Writing Centers at NYU and Fairfield U.

As a freelancer, she leads book group discussions, teaches writing workshops, and writes about books. She is also the founder and editor of Books, Ink at HamletHub, a website on all things books.

ABOUT THE ILLUSTRATOR

Ha Pham is a designer and illustrator who discovered her passion for art as a child and taught herself to draw. After graduating from Hanoi University of Industrial Fine Arts in Vietnam, she worked as a freelancer designing logos, graphics, and promotional printing campaigns for companies **around the world.**

With passion and commitment, she loves creating art that everyone loves and finds useful for life. She can be contacted at haphamthu08@gmail.com.